WHO IS THIS JESUS?

BIBLE
MODULAR
SERIES

BJU PRESS

GREENVILLE, SOUTH CAROLINA

This textbook was written by members of the faculty and staff of Bob Jones University. Standing for the "old-time religion" and the absolute authority of the Bible since 1927, Bob Jones University is the world's leading Fundamentalist Christian university. The staff of the University is devoted to educating Christian men and women to be servants of Jesus Christ in all walks of life.

Providing unparalleled academic excellence, Bob Jones University prepares its students through its offering of over one hundred majors, while its fervent spiritual emphasis prepares their minds and hearts for service and devotion to the Lord Jesus Christ.

If you would like more information about the spiritual and academic opportunities available at Bob Jones University, please call
1-800-BJ-AND-ME (1-800-252-6363).
www.bju.edu

NOTE:

The fact that materials produced by other publishers may be referred to in this volume does not constitute an endorsement by BJU Press of the content or theological position of materials produced by such publishers. The position of BJU Press, and of Bob Jones University, is well known. Any references and ancillary materials are listed as an aid to the student or the teacher and in an attempt to maintain the accepted academic standards of the publishing industry.

Who Is This Jesus?

Thomas Parr, M.A.
Bryan Smith, Ph.D.

Project Editor: Elizabeth Bang Berg
Designer: Dan Van Leeuwen
Cover Designer: Cory Godbey
Compositor: Jennifer Hearing
Illustrators: John Bjerk, Matt Bjerk, Cory Godbey, Preston Gravely Jr., Chris Koelle, and Dave Schuppert

Photo credits appear on page 155.

© 2004 BJU Press
Greenville, South Carolina 29614

Printed in the United States of America

ISBN 1-57924-963-9

15 14 13 12 11 10 9 8 7 6 5 4 3 2 1

CONTENTS

He saith unto them, **But whom say ye that I am?**

And Simon Peter answered and said, Thou art **the Christ,** the **Son** of the living **God.**

And Jesus answered and said unto him, **Blessed** art **thou,** Simon Bar-jona: for flesh and blood hath not revealed it unto thee, but my **Father** which is in heaven.

Matthew 16:15–17

Introduction

Memory Verses: Matthew 16:15–17

I love books. I always have, even before I could read. So I guess it shouldn't surprise you when I say that sometimes I go to the library for no apparent reason. Well, actually, it's not the library that I really like. My favorite place for books and reading is Homer's. No, that's not the owner's name. His name is Jim. He calls his bookstore *Homer's* because he hopes that it's the kind of place that someone like Homer (you know, the guy who wrote the *Iliad* and the *Odyssey*) would enjoy. If the grandfather of Western literature would like it, Jim says, then it must be a whiz-banger of a bookstore.

Anyway, that's where this story begins—and stays really. It was a Thursday afternoon. I had just turned in a huge project at school, I had nothing due the next day, and I needed a place to unwind as a sort of reward for all my hard work. So I walked in and headed straight for the classics. I knew exactly what I wanted. *Dickens.* There's nothing quite like cuddling up in one of Jim's old beat-up chairs with a story about some "poor old chap" who overcame prejudice and poverty—especially when I've just overcome some nasty thing.

What am I doing sitting and reading a book in a bookstore? Well, that's just the kind of place Homer's is. It's not simply a *buying* bookstore; it's a *reading* bookstore (of course, with all the money I've spent there, Jim could probably start a national chain). You go, plop down with a book, and let yourself get transported into another world. Homer's is the perfect place for that kind of thing. It's not like a library—sterile, academic, and sort of deadening.

1

It's got *character.* The musty smells, the uneven floors, the piles of old books everywhere—it all makes Homer's the perfect doorway for an imagination hungry for a journey.

But on that particular Thursday afternoon, there was no journey. Walking through the religion section on my way to Dickens, I got stopped by a certain book that was sticking out from the shelf. It had a fire-engine red cover—couldn't miss it if I had tried. It said on the spine, *Learn to Know and Love God.* Seems like Pastor is always talking about getting closer to God—so much so that I find myself thinking about it a lot. So when I saw that title, I picked up the book and started reading.

"The problem with most people is that they are not rightly related to God" (page 1). *Boy, that's the truth,* I thought as I kept skimming.

"We all have to face the fact that other people are not to blame for our unhappiness—we are" (page 3). *Don't I know people who need to hear that!*

"In the final analysis, we must conclude that all the world's woe is the result of *sin.* But the good news is that God loves us and is willing to forgive us" (page 4). *Amen. Preach it!*

Well, by that time I was really wanting to know who the author was. So I shut the book and started scanning the back cover. That's when I got my big surprise.

> The author of this book, Gordon Decker, was converted to the Church of Jesus Christ of Latter-day Saints at the age of twenty. He has authored many tracts and booklets advocating Mormonism.

"A *Mormon!* What in the world?!" I said, not realizing how loud my outburst was.

"What's the matter—didn't you realize you were reading from the Mormonism shelf?" Jim asked me, not even looking up from his shelving.

Sure enough, there was the sign. *Mormonism.* It was written in that clumsy handwriting that seems to stand for everything I know about Jim. He's a mess. He's short, fat, unkempt, and hairy.

He's got hair everywhere—on his arms, on his face, in his ears. Everywhere, that is, but on the top of his head. But, believe it or not, all of that is kind of endearing. I guess it's because, despite it all, Jim is friendly, very friendly. And he's also extremely smart. So mess or not, he's the kind of person it's hard not to like.

"I can't believe a Mormon wrote this," I said, still stunned by my discovery.

"Why not? They're good religious people too." Jim is nice, but he's not a churchgoer. All religions look the same to him.

"Well, I'm sure they're religious. I just didn't think that their religious beliefs were so close to my own. I mean, I skimmed through several pages, and I didn't find a thing that would sound strange at my church on a Sunday morning."

"And this bothers you?" With this question Jim stopped what he was doing and turned to look at me.

"Of course it does. Mormons are weird. Their religion is kooky."

"Steve, Steve, Steve." *Steve* is my name, by the way. "That's a pretty condemning statement. How many books on Mormonism have you read?"

"Uh . . . none."

"I think if you'll look into it, you'll find that there's much more that you agree with in Mormonism than you disagree with. In fact, I'd be willing to say that about any religion."

"Hmm. You never struck me as a religion expert."

"Well, these are all my books, aren't they?" Jim said as he went back to shelving.

"Aw, c'mon, Jim. That doesn't mean you've read them all."

"Of course not. But I've read a lot more of them than you'd probably think. And I'm convinced that all religions teach basically the same thing—*there is a God; He made us; if we trust in Him, He'll take us to heaven.* Each one says it differently, but they're all pointing in the same direction. That's why I stock so many religious books from so many different religions.

3

That's why there's a Judaism shelf, a Jehovah's Witnesses shelf, a Mormonism shelf, and an Islam shelf. In fact, Steve, one of the reasons Homer's exists is to show people what you're just now discovering—there are many ways to God, and we shouldn't judge others for trying a path we've chosen not to take."

"Well, that's Jim's opinion, Steve. And if you ask me, it ain't worth much." That was Jenny's voice, coming from behind the shelf that Jim was stocking. Jenny is nobody's dummy. She's a junior at the university that's about forty minutes from our town. I don't think she's ever gotten anything lower than an *A-* in any-thing—and that includes P.E. She's smart, spunky, organized, and she's an outspoken Christian. I guess you could say that she's everything Jim isn't. Except for the smart thing; they both have brains twice the size of mine. And they're both friendly. Anyway, she's worked at Homer's for two or three years, and I dare say she's the main reason that Jim's messy way of life hasn't torpe-doed his attempts at running his own business.

"Sounds like my favorite heretic has overheard yet another one of my conversations," Jim fired off, good-naturedly, of course.

"Well, Jim, if you're as committed to balance and accuracy in the interaction of ideas as you always say you are, you can't fault me for trying to moderate your extreme views."

"*I'm* trying to moderate *Steve's* extreme views."

"He's extreme because he dares to think that somebody else is wrong?! C'mon. Claiming that everybody is right . . . now *that's* extreme." Told you she had spunk.

"I don't think that everybody is right. I just feel that Steve needs to—"

" 'I'm convinced that all religions teach basically the same thing,' " she quoted Jim. "That's pretty extreme if you ask me. Some people kill in the name of religion, while others sacrifice themselves for their fellow man in the name of religion. How dare you insult the latter by equating them with the former!"

"So, Jenny, do you lie awake at night thinking of combative things to say to me?"

"Nope. Just comes natural," she said, finally coming out from behind the shelf with a big grin on her face.

"OK," I said. "I'm satisfied that my views have been adequately defended. If you don't mind, I'm going to go do what I came for. Read some Dickens."

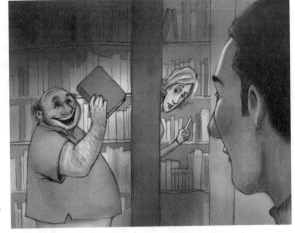

"Ah, but Steve," Jim smiled, "your views have not been defended."

"That's true," Jenny added. "All I did was defend my opinion of Jim's opinion. I don't know how anyone could defend your judgment of Mormonism when you yourself have never researched Mormonism."

"Well, I am indeed ashamed of myself. OK, folks, it's like this—I came here to relax because I've been thinking too much for too long. So, if you don't mind, I'm going to stop thinking and start relaxing."

"So you'd rather give yourself to things you've thought about many times already, like Dickens, than give yourself to something new?" As you can tell, Jenny gets under my skin.

"Yup. I guess so." I've learned that a person has a much better chance of matching wills with Jenny than he does matching wits.

"Jim, are you thinking what I'm thinking?" she said, looking straight into his eyes.

"I think so."

"It's been a long time, hasn't it?"

"Too long, way too long."

"Too long for what?" I hate having my curiosity manipulated.

"We've gone too long without an *Auseinandersetzung!*" Jim almost yelled, throwing both arms up in the air.

"Ousenander—what?!"

"It's pronounced *ows ine ON der zets unk,*" Jenny said slowly and deliberately. Then she scribbled the word on a piece of paper, complete with its pronunciation. "It's a German word that refers to a vigorous discussion of ideas. We have them every now and then for certain preferred patrons. If one of our customers is interested in a particular controversial topic, we get a bunch of 'experts' together (we call them the *Fachmänner*) who can discuss their points of view at length."

"I don't know." I was feeling really queasy by this time. "I just don't think I know enough—"

"That's the point of an Auseinandersetzung," Jim said before I could finish. "You don't know enough about a particular topic (in this case, the beliefs of competing world religions), so we have the Fachmänner get together to argue about their views in front of you, and you get a better idea of what you should think."

"Yes, but I don't think I know enough about this stuff to follow what they'll say."

"Well, good night, Steve! You've gone to church every week for years. Haven't you learned anything about religion during that time?"

"Aw, cool it, Jim," Jenny said. "Steve, you'll do fine. Besides, I'll be sure to be here. I've sat through several of these, so I know how they go. And I would love to be part of one on world religions. The last one we had was about the morality of continued dependence on fossil fuels. The discussion was interesting, but it was nothing compared to what this could be. This will be totally cool. Furthermore, Steve, if you're serious about being a Christian, how could you turn down this golden opportunity? You'll have a chance to examine what other faiths teach and contrast them to the teachings of the Bible."

Well, what do you say to something like that? Now I couldn't even match wills with Jenny. "OK. But I do have some conditions.

First, nobody puts me on the spot. You can't let some wacko convince me to get baptized in sauerkraut—or something like that. Second, one of the experts has to be an educated, knowledgeable Christian."

"Granted," Jim answered. "Now, what religions should we have represented?"

"Well, I've already mentioned Christianity. And I guess we have to do Mormonism, since that sort of got this whole thing going. Uh . . . I suppose the religions here on these shelves would be good. That'd be Islam, the Jehovah's Witnesses, and Judaism. Does that sound OK?"

"Perfect. Here's how we'll do it. I'll get on the phone tomorrow morning and contact our experts. We'll plan on meeting five times, one night for each religion, over the next couple of weeks. If all goes well, we should be able to have our first Auseinandersetzung on Monday night, after Homer's closes. I'll call you, Steve, to confirm, but for now plan on being here at seven o'clock Monday."

"OK." I swallowed hard.

Jim and Jenny then exchanged high-fives, shouting "Auseinandersetzung!" with each smack of their hands. Things were different for me. I slid back into the classics and wandered to my Dickens spot. I found a copy of *Bleak House* and started reading. Didn't work, though. I was too concerned about what was happening in my world to have the energy to enter Dickens's.

Evidently all went well for Jim on Friday. When I got home from school, I found his message on the answering machine saying that we had a green light for the meeting.

As I drove to Homer's Monday evening, I found myself wondering if maybe the whole thing had fallen apart over the weekend. Walking up the sidewalk, I even practiced acting surprised and disappointed should Jim greet me with the news that everything was off. That's when I opened the front door. *Rats!* There they all were—the five Fachmänner flanked by Jim and Jenny.

"Welcome, Steve," Jim said as he walked toward me, ready to shake my hand. "Experts, this is our Sucher." (It was pronounced *ZOO kher,* with the *kh* being a throaty sort of a sound that made you think someone was about to spit.)

"Our what?!" I asked.

"*Sucher,* Steve. It means 'seeker.' This is an Auseinandersetzung, these are the Fachmänner, and you are the honored Sucher. Speaking of Fachmänner, let me introduce each of them to you."

It appeared that everything was going to happen in the main reading area, the open space just to the left of the front door. It's furnished with living-room furniture from the 1970s. In the center there's a long coffee table. In front of the table sits a big pea-green couch with more holes and rips in it than in a sunken Spanish warship. Opposite the couch, on the other side of the table, there are a loveseat and an armchair, both in pretty good shape. The loveseat's a rust color (not the sort of thing you see much anymore), and the armchair is yellow. Then at each end of the coffee table is an armchair—both orange.

Jim took me to each Fachmann (I later learned that was the singular of *Fachmänner*). "Steve, this is Hamid. I've known him for quite some time. He's a professor of Persian and Arabic literature at the university not far from here. He'll be helping us with Islam."

"Greetings. I'm looking forward to dispelling a number of common myths about Islam," he said in an impressively deep voice and with a noticeable accent. His voice made me expect him to sell me lots of oil, or maybe a camel. His appearance was very ordinary, however. Well, it wasn't *completely* ordinary. He wasn't wearing jeans and a turtleneck, like I was. He wore a white shirt and navy dress pants. He looked like Pastor on a day off. But he looked a lot older than Pastor. Hamid was not young. He had gray hair and a gray, closely cropped beard. I'd say he was about sixty-five.

"Now I want you to meet Shlomo," Jim said (the name is pronounced just as it looks—a little weird, I know). "He just moved to our area after finishing his seminary studies at Yeshiva University. He's a rabbi, and he'll be representing Judaism."

Shlomo looked somewhere between twenty-five and thirty. He was the only one wearing a hat. Well, it wasn't really a hat. It was more like one of those really old, small baseball caps— without the bill.

"Do you like my yarmulke? You keep staring at it," Shlomo said with a forgiving smile.

"Sorry about that. I was wondering what it was called," I said with some embarrassment.

"Don't be sorry. I wear it so people will notice that I'm different. As an Orthodox Jew, I am part of the oldest monotheistic religion in the world."

Well, he certainly smoothed that over pretty well. Even so, Shlomo did seem a bit nervous. He didn't have the same calm, confident composure that Hamid seemed to have.

"Now, Steve, I want you to meet Javier," Jim said. "He'll be our Jehovah's Witness. He's been an elder at a nearby Kingdom Hall for the last twelve years."

"Pleased to meet you," I said. It seemed strange to me that though I had spent a great deal of energy trying to avoid Jehovah's Witnesses in my neighborhood, I was now about to invite one to talk with me at length.

"Thank you. I hope this is really beneficial for you." Javier appeared to be in his forties and was dark in complexion. For a few seconds we just stared at each other. I kept trying to imagine how he would look when he really "got going." He just kept staring at me with a strained smile. Mercifully, Jim moved me on to the next Fachmann after only a few seconds.

"Steve, this is Sean, a Mormon. He wasn't easy to get ahold of. Since the nearest LDS church is more than an hour away, I had to use the friend of a friend of a friend to bring him in. Thank you very much for coming, Sean."

"It's good to meet you, Steve," Sean began. "I trust that you will keep your mind open, but most of all I pray that you will keep your *heart* open," he said, tapping his chest with his right index figure. He sort of reminded me of my Uncle Gene, my mom's kid brother—thirty-something, tall, and skinny. Like Shlomo, he seemed nervous. No, he seemed more than nervous. I guess I'd say that he seemed distracted. Like this whole thing was bothering him more than it was me.

"OK, Steve, now for one of your own," Jim said, leading me to the only Fachmann left. "This is Donald. He's been coming to Homer's for as long as it's been here. You asked that the Christian be very knowledgeable, so I got you the best one I could think of. He's been a pastor and a seminary professor for over twenty years. We've had many a stimulating discussion here in this store, and I'm sure that he won't let you down."

"Steve, I've heard some good things about you. I suppose you already know what being a Christian is all about. But hope-fully this interaction will deepen your knowledge of the truth." Donald struck me as an odd combination. He was a big man: at least six feet tall, and probably two hundred pounds. But he wasn't young; he looked like he was in his mid fifties. And he didn't talk like a big guy. His voice was high baritone or tenor, and he had some kind of slight accent.

"You're not from around here, are you?" Another stupid thing to say, I know. I do that when I get nervous. That's just one reason I didn't want to do this thing.

"Well, that's pretty perceptive of you. No, I'm not from around here. I'm from Canada. But I've lived here for about as long as you've been alive, so I think I fit in pretty well."

"OK," Jim broke in and ended my little public-relations fiasco. "Now that we've all met, let's have a seat and get started. Steve and Jenny, you take the couch. Fachmänner, you take the other seats. Since I'm the moderator, I'll sit at the counter."

When Jim took his seat, he sat above everybody else because he was sitting on the stool that was behind the counter where people paid for their books. I sat on the side of the couch nearer Jim. Javier took the armchair just in front of the counter. Sean sat in the armchair opposite Javier, on the other side of the coffee table. And Donald sat in the one armchair that was left, the one beside the loveseat. All of this happened in a matter of seconds. Then we all noticed that the two still standing, who for some reason were especially slow at making a seat choice, were the most unlikely couple to occupy a loveseat together. When Hamid and Shlomo realized what the seating arrangements would be, it was definitely a "Kodak moment." They at first looked surprised, then embarrassed, and finally laughed one of those nervous laughs that have a humor of their own. Then they quietly sat down.

"Well, it looks like world peace is closer than any of us may have guessed," Jim said with a chuckle. "Now, let me lay down the ground rules for our Auseinandersetzung. First thing: I'm the moderator, which means that I'm in charge. If you have something to say and it's not your turn as a Fachmann, you must be recognized by me. Second thing: we're doing this primarily for Steve's sake, our Sucher. This means that the previous rule doesn't apply to him. He can talk whenever he wants, and he gets to choose who will cross-examine the Fachmann (and in what order) once the Fachmann's presentation is done. If Steve chooses, he can share this privilege with Jenny." Jim said this looking at me, as if he was expecting me to say something.

"Uh, yeah," I answered, when I realized everyone was looking at me. "I'll let Jenny have semi-Sucher status."

"Cool!" You can probably guess who said that.

"OK, Sucher, what order would you like to go in?" Jim asked.

"Umm, I guess we could go in chronological order. You know, the oldest religion first."

"That would be Judaism. Shlomo, you are the Fachmann of the hour," Jim announced. "You may begin."

Just a Man

1

"Yes, well, that is true. Judaism is the oldest of the religions represented here." Shlomo sat on the edge of his seat, partly because—I suppose—he wanted to get a little "elbow room."

"In fact," he continued, "each of the religions here ultimately must trace its lineage back to the religion of the Jews. Before Jesus of Nazareth was born, all who would later call themselves Christians were adherents of Judaism. Because they are considered offshoots of the Christian church, Mormons and Jehovah's Witnesses owe much of their ideas to Judaism as well. And Islam claims to trace its spiritual heritage back to Abraham. So I think it is very important at the beginning of my presentation to map out a brief history of Judaism.

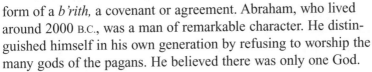

"The story of Judaism begins with Abraham, because it was with him that the divine-human encounter took the form of a *b'rith,* a covenant or agreement. Abraham, who lived around 2000 B.C., was a man of remarkable character. He distinguished himself in his own generation by refusing to worship the many gods of the pagans. He believed there was only one God.

"God took delight in this man of courage, and he entered into a b'rith with him. He told him to leave his home (Ur, which was located in modern southern Iraq) and that He would make him a great nation. In this b'rith, God made three specific promises. First, He told Abraham that he would have a very numerous 'seed,' or group of descendants. Second, He would give him and his descendants the land of Canaan (basically modern Israel) as an eternal possession. Both of these promises were simply the necessary components of the general promise to make him a great nation.

The History of the Jewish Faith

I. Biblical Judaism (2000–400 B.C.)
II. Hellenistic Judaism (400 B.C.–A.D. 150)
III. Rabbinic Judaism (150–1750)
IV. Modern Judaism (1750–present)

Any legitimate nation must be able to claim a group of people with a common heritage and culture, and it must have a land with clear boundaries where those people can live. To these two promises (the promises of a seed and of a land), God added a third: He promised to give a universal blessing to the peoples of the world through Abraham's descendants.

"Abraham obeyed and came to Canaan. But God did not fulfill His promises right away. In time God miraculously gave him a son, Isaac, but Abraham never came to possess Canaan. He died with only one son of promise, Isaac. In time Isaac had Jacob, later called Israel. And when Jacob was grown, God gave him twelve sons. These twelve sons, often called the twelve patriarchs, were the foundation of the nation of Israel. The nation would one day be divided into twelve tribes, according to these patriarchs' names.

"But it was not in Canaan that Abraham's seed became numerous. While Jacob was still alive, he and his family moved to Egypt to escape a famine. Though at first they were treated well, in time Jacob's descendants were enslaved by the Egyptians. They remained there for over four centuries, during which time their situation only worsened. Yet it was in the midst of this slavery that the descendants of Israel (Jacob) became a great company of people. At the time of their deliverance, they probably numbered more than two million.

"It was at the end of these four hundred years in Egypt that perhaps the greatest descendant of Abraham was born—Moses. It was with the birth and coming of age of Moses that the God of promise became the God of fulfillment. He used Moses to bring ten horrific plagues on the Egyptians. The plagues convinced Pharaoh to let Israel leave. Moses then led Israel to Mount Sinai, where God forged them into a nation worthy of His name."

"And how did He do that?" I asked.

"He gave them *torah*. This is a Hebrew word that most translate as 'law.' That translation is a bit misleading, however. The word comes from a Hebrew verb meaning 'to teach.' There in the desert God taught the people how to think as His special nation, how to live in harmony with their fellow citizens, how to raise their families properly, and—most importantly—how to worship Him as He desired. The *Torah* (with a capital *T*) comprises the books of Genesis, Exodus, Leviticus, Numbers, and Deuteronomy. This is the ultimate source of divine instruction for Jews. This is the reason that Moses is such an important figure in Jewish history. He gave us the Torah."

"So what exactly does the Torah teach?" Jenny asked.

"Well, since you are a Christian, you should be familiar with it," Shlomo said with a broad smile.

"Yes, but how do *you* summarize its contents?"

"Basically, the essence of the Torah is expressed in the Ten Commandments. They tell the Jews about their obligation to God and their obligation to their fellow man."

"OK, but it seems with your understanding of history, God is concerned only for Jews. What about other peoples and nations? I mean, God's third promise to Abraham was that he would somehow be a blessing to the entire world, right?" I thought that was a natural question for a Gentile to ask.

"Yes, God charged Israel at Sinai to accept and follow His torah so that they could be 'a kingdom of priests and a holy nation.' By this He meant that they would be His agents, bringing the entire world back into a right relationship with Him."

"And they agreed to this?" I asked.

"Yes, and it was at that moment—there at the foot of Mount Sinai—that the descendants of Israel became *Israel,* the chosen nation. But many sad days lay ahead. Israel said it would obey God's torah, but it did not. The God of Israel was, however, faithful to His b'rith with Abraham. He had promised to make him a mighty nation, and He did not change His mind. Through a series of fascinating events, He gave them King David.

"The kingship of David marks a very important point in the history of my people. It was at this time that the Jewish doctrine of *Messiah* (which means 'the anointed one') became more clearly defined and became part of the nation's identity. It is not until this period that we learn the Messiah would be a son of David and that through Him Israel would stand forever.

"David was not the Messiah, nor was his son Solomon. Solomon had many good qualities, but in the end he was an idolater. Beginning with him the nation embarked on a slow, tragic slide to ruin. It took some time (two-and-a-half centuries for one part of the nation and three-and-a-half for the other), but God dealt with His people severely. He temporarily reversed His b'rith. He took the Promised Land away and scattered them among the nations.

"I should mention that during this long period of decline, another significant portion of Scripture was written, the *Neviim* (or the Prophets). Now when I say 'the Prophets,' I mean something different from what you're probably thinking of. The historical books, Joshua through Kings (with the exception of Ruth), as well as the prophetical books, are considered to be books of prophecy. That's because Jews considered their inspired historians to be fulfilling the same basic role as their prophets—they both warned Israel that judgment was unavoidable for those who forsook God's instruction. But there was more to the Neviim than judgment. Messianic expectation reaches a crescendo, especially among the Major and Minor Prophets. There the Messiah is presented as a mighty Redeemer who will come to restore Israel to her former glory and who will bring peace to all nations, teaching them to live by torah.

"But Israel did not listen to these prophets, and they therefore were sent into exile. After seventy years, however, God brought them back—again, an evidence that He would not forsake His

---

Tanakh

Torah
Law
Genesis, Exodus
Leviticus, Numbers
Deuteronomy

Neviim
Former Prophets
Joshua, Judges
I & II Samuel
I & II Kings
Latter Prophets
Isaiah, Jeremiah
Ezekiel, Hosea
Joel, Amos
Obadiah, Jonah
Micah, Nahum
Habakkuk
Zephaniah
Haggai, Zechariah
Malachi

Ketuvim
Writings
Psalms, Proverbs
Job, Song of Solomon
Ruth, Lamentations
Ecclesiastes
Esther, Daniel
Ezra, Nehemiah
I & II Chronicles

b'rith with Abraham. During this post-exilic period, probably the most important person for the subsequent history of Judaism was the scribe Ezra. He was a very influential teacher of torah during the 400s B.C. He compiled and organized the final section of the Hebrew Scriptures, the *Ketuvim* (or the Writings). With his work the foundation of Judaism was laid. Today, Jews call these Scriptures the *Tanakh,* which is an acronym for the names of its three main sections: *T*orah, *N*eviim, and *K*etuvim.

"I would call the period I've just covered (from 2000 to 400 B.C.) *Biblical Judaism,* since this was the period in which the Tanakh (or the Old Testament, as Christians call it) was produced. The next period I would call *Hellenistic Judaism*. This period lasted from about 400 B.C. to roughly A.D. 150. The distinguishing characteristic of this time was the Jews' struggle to know how to respond to Greek culture. Because of the conquests of Alexander the Great (in the late 300s B.C.), the land of the Jews was invaded by Greek culture. Some believed it was fine to Hellenize (live like the Greeks). But others said that Hellenizing was a return to the idolatry that led to Israel's exile several centuries earlier.

"In time all realized the dangers of Hellenization. The Jews revolted but were crushed by the Romans in A.D. 70, and their city and temple were destroyed. About fifty years later, the Jews tried to revolt again, but then the consequences were even more severe. The Jews were driven out of their land. Israel was no longer a nation, not even a servile nation. And circumcision and torah instruction were forbidden. Judaism seemed dead."

"Wait. Haven't you forgotten something?" I asked. "You haven't said anything about Jesus." I looked at Jenny for reassurance, and she started pumping her head, indicating I was right to ask that question.

"Jesus of Nazareth is not as important to the history of Judaism as you apparently think. *Yes,* He was a Jew, and *yes,* He lived during the first century A.D. But outside the record of what you call the New Testament, we basically know nothing about Him. He personally is not important to this history. Only His followers and what they said He said are important. Now, let's see, where was I?"

"Judaism was dead," I replied coolly.

"Ah yes, or it *seemed* dead, rather. What followed was a long period commonly known as *Rabbinic Judaism* (from 150 to 1750). This was a millennium and a half of exile and ostracism. Without

A modern-day synagogue

a land to live in and without a temple to worship in, Judaism faced a long exile. Whereas Judaism once looked to kings and priests for leadership and instruction, they now looked to the rabbis. The *rabbi* (the word means 'my master') was a teacher of torah who encouraged fellow Jews to pursue quiet piety through prayer, good deeds, and study of the Tanakh. Synagogues replaced the temple as the center of Jewish worship. But confidence in the b'rith remained. The Jews still looked for the Messiah. In fact, I think their messianic hopes were greater now because they were looking for the Messiah not only to come and fix the world's problems but also to make them Israel again.

"Now since the Torah no longer directly addressed their situation, the rabbis worked to produce the *Mishnah* ('repetition'), a collection of Jewish oral traditions that helped to clarify the meaning of the Torah and its many laws.

"As time passed, many Jews found that often even the Mishnah was not specific enough. So eventually the *Gemara* ('completion') was added to the Mishnah. Together, the Mishnah and the Gemara became known as the *Talmud* ('learning')."

"OK, I've heard of that." I was glad to finally hear something that sounded familiar.

"Yes, I'm sure you have. The Talmud and the Tanakh are sacred to all faithful Jews. Armed with these two books, the Jews were ready for the long, difficult centuries of the Middle Ages.

"The story of Judaism in the Middle Ages is a story of pain and persecution," Shlomo continued. "Medieval culture was dominated by two religions that were very unfriendly to Judaism: Christianity and Islam. Christians hated Jews because they thought of them as 'Christ killers.' Muslims hated Jews because they refused to recognize Muhammad as God's greatest prophet.

"Jews who were scattered from India to Spain faced riots, massacres, and expulsions. Many Jews, especially in eastern Europe, dealt with their misery by feeding messianic hopes. The Jews were an abused and despairing people."

"OK now, Shlomo, earlier you said that this whole period— I think you called it Rabbinic Judaism—ended around 1750. So what happened at that time that brought this huge period to a close?" Jenny was evidently trying to keep things moving along.

"Yes, well, the period from 1750 to the present we may call *Modern Judaism,* and what makes it different is two things working together. First, in the mid 1700s a series of laws was passed in Europe, freeing Jews from governmental persecution. Second, with the profound disappointment resulting from dashed messianic hopes, many Jews began to realize that they had to start taking responsibility for their own well-being. So Jews throughout Europe began actively pursuing—and they could now that persecution had been lifted—fulfillment on this earth.

"Now, let me hasten to add that although the overall trend was away from persecution, Jewish persecution did continue. Indeed, the worst Russian pogroms were yet to come."

"Pogroms?"

"A *pogrom* usually refers to an organized, state-sponsored massacre or persecution of Jews. The worst ones were in 1881. But that is another story. Of greater significance to the history of Judaism is the Haskala movement that transformed Judaism worldwide. *Haskala* is Hebrew for 'enlightenment.' Jews claimed to 'see the light' regarding Gentile culture. Haskala Jews wanted to be thoroughly integrated into Gentile society. This was not a bad thing, not in essence anyway. Some, however, did go too far, and I believe Reform Jews are among them.

"Fascinated by the philosophies and scientific developments of the Gentiles during the Age of Reason, Reform Judaism (which started in the 1800s) denied that any part of the Tanakh or Talmud was divine revelation. It was all the work of men, and it therefore was not binding. Reform Jews ignore the dietary laws of the Torah, they don't necessarily circumcise their children, and they don't even require that their children marry within the Jewish faith. Initially, this kind of Judaism was very popular. By the end of the 1800s almost all of the synagogues in America were Reform. But throughout the twentieth century, it lost ground. And it's not hard to see why. If you reject the foundation of Judaism, you have no real reason to remain a Jew. The children of Reform Jews often marry Christians. The result is grandchildren who don't even consider themselves Jewish.

Three Main Kinds of Judaism

Orthodox
Believes that the Tanakh and the Talmud are the inspired Word of God. Seeks to preserve historic Judaism by emphasizing adherence to ancient Jewish traditions.

Conservative
A mediating position between Orthodox and Reform Judaism. Believes that the Tanakh and the Talmud are from God but are not inspired in the traditional sense. Attempts to adapt the traditions of Judaism while maintaining its essential values.

Reform
Asserts that the Tanakh and the Talmud are of human origin and are valuable only for the moral guidance they give. Attempts to modernize Judaism by releasing Jews from the responsibility of keeping the Jewish rituals.

"Consequently, early in the twentieth century Conservative Judaism began. Conservative Judaism believes that both the Tanakh and the Talmud are from God. Therefore, they believe that a Jew must keep all the laws in the Torah that are possible at this time. They differ from Orthodox Jews, however, in that they feel free to apply those laws in ways that Jews have not done historically. So on the surface, Conservative Jews *look* much more like Reform Jews than they do Orthodox Jews. But they *believe* much more like the Orthodox."

"And what about the Orthodox?" I asked.

"Orthodox Judaism is traditional Judaism. We believe that the holy books of Judaism are divine revelation. We also believe that the laws of the Tanakh are to be obeyed. Some say, 'But times change, and Torah observance must change too.' While I agree that that statement is true to a degree, I have found that most Jews who use it just want to excuse their own unwillingness to obey God. Times don't change the Torah, but the Torah can change the times. I should mention, however, that there are many different types of Orthodox Judaism. Some of them are very strict, such as the Hasadim and the Haredim. Other types are much more moderate, including the Modern Orthodox."

"And you?"

"I consider myself a Modern Orthodox. I believe in diligently studying and observing the Torah. But I also believe that one can study the Torah and admire Gentile culture. Secular professions, art, and literature can all be part of a Jew's life. If you want a symbol in American Judaism of this, look at my alma mater, Yeshiva University, located in New York City. Its motto is *Torah u'Madda*—'Torah and secular learning.' Properly understood, that captures the essence of Modern Orthodoxy.

"Now I would like to discuss the two most important events for Judaism from the twentieth century, the Holocaust and the founding of the state of Israel. Six million Jews were—"

"Hold on," Jim interrupted Shlomo. "You've spent enough time talking about Jewish history. I think we all pretty much know about those two events. But we really do need to move on. Can you please discuss Jewish doctrine and practice?"

"Um, well, please understand that I would prefer not to skip over these important events"—Shlomo glanced nervously at Jim, who was glaring at him—"but of course I realize I do need to discuss Jewish beliefs. I should mention that what I'm about to outline does not describe all of present-day Judaism, only Orthodox Judaism.

"It should not surprise you to discover that the three main headings of Jewish doctrine (at least as I'm presenting them here) have each been discussed somewhat already in my presentation. These headings are *God*, *man*, and the *b'rith*.

"Central to the Jewish idea of God is the most important state-ment to be found in the Torah: *Shema Yisrael Adonai Elohenu, Adonai Ehad*. I quote it to you in Hebrew because that is how we recite it during each Sabbath synagogue service. It means, 'Hear,

O Israel, the Lord our God; the Lord is one' (which is from Deuteronomy 6:4). Everything that Jews believe about the Supreme Being
is found in that brief statement, albeit in seed form.

"The first thing that it tells us is that this Being is *one*. This
observation communicates two important ideas. First, there is
only one God. It was this discovery that distinguished Abraham
from others in his generation. It is ironic that the influence of
Judaism in this regard has been so powerful that it no longer dis-
tinguishes Judaism. Most religious people today are monotheists:
they believe there is only one God. But this brings me to my
second point about divine oneness. Deuteronomy 6:4 does still
distinguish the Jews from other religions, especially Christianity,
because it affirms that God is unified and singular in His person.
In other words, there is no Trinity in Jewish theology. Everywhere
in the Tanakh—which you too take as divine revelation—the Lord
is presented as without partners.

"If God is one, how can He be three? It is by definition a contradiction. Also, this teaching humanizes God. The Christian doctrine of the incarnation, which is an implication of the doctrine of
the Trinity, teaches that the second person of the Godhead became
a man. What an insult! The eter-
nal, indescribable God became
a finite being, subject to human
limitations and suffering?! What
is even more deplorable is that
Christians teach that Jesus as
God *died*. This is absurd—that God could die. But what is most
disturbing is the idea that man needs a mediator between God and
himself. As Jews we believe what God said at Sinai: "I am the
Lord, *your God*" (which comes from Exodus 20:2). The God of
the Jews is not distant, unwilling to come into contact with His
worshipers until persuaded by a mediator. He is *our* God. We do
not need someone else to pray for us, live for us, or die for us."

By this time my eyes were wide open—not because I was mad,
just scared. I thought lightning was about to strike. Then I shot a
glance at Jim. He looked totally unaffected by what had been said.
Strange, given his belief about all religions being the same.

> *We do not need someone
> else to pray for us, live
> for us, or die for us.*
> ~Shlomo

"I think I see where you're coming from," I said, trying to get my thoughts together. "So what do you think about Jesus?"

"I think Jesus was a great man. His moral teaching and humble example remain among the most remarkable features of human history. But I refuse to believe what Christians insist I must—that Jesus of Nazareth is really Jesus of heaven. He showed people how to be more like God, but I deny that Jesus was God Himself."

I think Jesus was a great man. . . . But I deny that Jesus was God.

~Shlomo

"And what else does Deuteronomy 6:4 teach?" Jenny asked.

"It reveals that the Supreme Being is both Elohim as well as Adonai. These are the two titles for God that appear in the verse. *Elohim* is usually translated as 'God,' and it presents God as the supreme, all-powerful Creator of the universe. There is no one like Him. It also presents Him as the Judge of all the earth. He is the omnipotent and omniscient Ruler of the universe. He does what is right. All who obey Him will be rewarded, and all who do not will be punished. But there is more to the character of God than His being Elohim. He is also *Adonai,* often translated 'Lord.' This word presents God as near, caring, and compassionate. As Adonai He is careful to meet His creatures' needs. He takes no delight in death and suffering—even when they are deserved. He is grieved because He loves all His creatures. This title also presents Him as one who delights to engage His special creature, man, in a personal relationship with Himself.

"Now let's turn our attention to Judaism's teaching regarding mankind. The most important point concerning my belief regarding man is what the Torah's first chapter states repeatedly about him—*man is made in God's own image.* What exactly that means has been debated for centuries, and I do not want you to think that what I believe is what all Jews believe.

"First of all, I think that when Genesis 1 says that man is made in God's image, it means that *man has God's reasoning capacity.* Unlike the animals, who live by instinct, men and women have intelligent minds that can think and reason, which enables us to interact with God. Because we can think like Him, we can talk to Him in prayer, and He can talk to us by our study of His Word.

"Second, the image of God in man implies that *we are essentially spirit beings.* We are much more than flesh and blood. We, like God, are spirits, and we, like God, will live forever. Yes, our bodies will die, but it is instinctive for all of us to expect something beyond that day of death. I believe that this instinct is a manifestation of the image of God in us.

"Third, because we are made in His image, *we are free moral agents.* By this I mean that we are free to choose between right and wrong. We never 'have to' sin. We may be tempted, but when we face temptation, we have within ourselves the image of God that can enable us to choose what God wants.

"Fourth, since we are made in the image of the supremely good Being in the universe, *we are essentially good ourselves.* Here again I disagree with the teachings of Christianity. Your apostle Paul claimed that all mankind became evil because of Adam's sin. Therefore, all people are basically evil. I find no support for this in the Jewish Scriptures, and I find the teaching repugnant. It makes God an ogre: how is it just for God to say that we are guilty because of what another man did? It also convinces people that they are incapable of doing what God commands them to do. God commands us to do good because we are like Him in His goodness and we are therefore able to do good. I think Christians would be better Christians if they would begin each day with the prayer that begins each Jew's day: 'My God, the soul you placed within me is pure. You created it, you fashioned it, you breathed it into me.' By the way, this point is not debated in Judaism. Jews everywhere affirm that man is essentially good, not evil.

God commands us to do good because we are . . . able to do good.

~Shlomo

"Finally, I should mention that because man is made in God's image, man's calling is a calling to *tikun olam.* These two words mean 'the repairing of the world.' When God made the world, He left it incomplete. Certainly, He could have made it flawless, but He chose not to because He wanted His prize creation—mankind—

to participate with Him in its completion. How He wishes for man to participate with Him in the tikun olam leads me to my next and final main point."

"The b'rith, right?"

"Ah yes, you have been listening. Very good, Sucher. As we have already mentioned, the b'rith is God's covenant with man. More specifically, it is His promise to Abraham to make from him a great and mighty nation."

"By giving him many descendants and by giving him the land of Canaan for those descendants to live in," Jenny inserted.

"Yes, and as I can see, you've been listening too. But the b'rith is not for the descendants of Abraham alone. God also promised in Genesis 12:3, 'In thee shall all families of the earth be blessed.' The b'rith is God's chosen means whereby He allows mankind to participate in tikun olam."

"OK, hold on," I said. "What does God's promise to Abraham have to do with everyone working together with God to fix the world?"

"The b'rith expresses God's plan for tikun olam in seed form. God gave Abraham His b'rith so that He could make from him Israel. He made Israel so that He could give this nation His torah. He gave them His torah so that they might know how to be a kingdom of priests. He wanted them to be a kingdom of priests so that they might—by the uniqueness of their lives and teaching— call all other nations to join them in their tikun olam. Then and only then could the goal of the b'rith be realized: 'In thee shall all families of the earth be blessed.' "

"OK, so it seems that the thing that's really central in this scheme is this whole idea of torah because—"

"Exactly!" To my surprise Shlomo was more than excited. He seemed beside himself with joy. "The game is won or lost on that point. If we heed God's instruction, we move forward in tikun olam. If we ignore it, we drift behind. It is the dynamic that makes the b'rith work. God's special instruction to the Jews is torah, teaching them how to love God and man. When everyone loves God and man as he should, the world will be repaired—creation will finally be complete. How this is done is stated most simply in the Ten Commandments. Now, of course, the other parts of the Torah expand on this a great deal. For example, they reveal that loving God affects the food we eat, the clothing we wear, what exactly we do on Saturday (the Sabbath), and so on."

"OK," I said, "Judaism throughout its history has seemed pretty self-absorbed. How is Judaism supposed to serve as a priest to all nations?"

"I would say that one of the main purposes of Judaism is to make *proselytes*. A proselyte is a convert. Jews should persuade people of different faiths to become Jews."

"But what about the Messiah?" Jenny asked. "It seems that He has been far more important to Judaism historically than He is to you in your current understanding."

"The Messiah is very important to the accomplishment of the tikun olam. The Tanakh reveals that the Messiah will be David's ultimate successor and that He will be the Jews' ideal ruler. Beyond that it's hard to say what role the Messiah will play. God has promised to send Him, so I am confident He will come. But anything more specific is speculation, and I don't like to speculate because that can get us into trouble. Judaism has had a problem with expecting too much from the Messiah. Jews have often retreated from difficulties and found comfort in the thought of the Messiah coming and making everything OK. In His own time, God will send the Messiah. In the meantime, we need to make sure that we're doing all we're supposed to do. We need to live worthy of the Messiah's leadership."

"OK, Shlomo's done," Jim said without giving the rabbi an opportunity to disagree. "I think now's a good time for us to get a stretch. I know if I don't move around some, I'll turn to stone. Sucher, in about ten minutes, you can have the other Fachmänner begin the cross examination."

Can Judaism Make Sense of Itself?

2

Memory Verses: Romans 10:3–4

It was good to get up and move around. I'd been sitting for a long time, and I felt like my head was in a fog. But walking around didn't seem to help much, not initially at least. So I went over to the water fountain and drank as much as I could. I don't know; it seemed that if I could just get my brain wet, I could keep going. When I turned around, I saw Jenny.

"I think congratulations are in order, Steve."

"For what?"

"For doing a very fine job at your first Auseinandersetzung. You felt like you couldn't do it, but as it turns out, you know more than you thought you did."

"Oh, I wouldn't say that. I think it's just—"

"OK, folks," Jim interrupted, "let's get back to our seats. It's time for the cross-examination."

As I walked back to the couch, I noticed Shlomo carrying a metal folding chair. *Not very comfortable,* I thought. Then I remembered how uncomfortable a loveseat could be when it's shared with someone of a rival religion. *Good thinking, Shlomo.*

"Sucher," Jim began, "you are in charge of choosing who will cross-examine the Fachmann. You may begin."

"I guess I'd like to get the Muslim perspective first. Hamid, what do you think of Shlomo's presentation?"

"I have nothing to say," he answered calmly with that distinctive accent of his.

"You don't have a problem with anything he said?" I asked.

"Oh, I did not say that. But most of my objections will come out naturally during my own presentation of my beliefs."

"Uh . . . sure. That's fine. Well, how about Sean?" I asked. "Sean, as a Mormon, what would you say to Shlomo?"

"I guess I'll start here, Shlomo," Sean said. "What are the limits of divine revelation, from your perspective? What books do you consider to be the inspired Word of God?"

"As I said before, the Tanakh and the Talmud are from God. The first is what God had His people write down, and the second is what He gave them to repeat orally from generation to generation. When the Jews ceased to exist as a nation, what had been oral had to be reduced to writing, and that's when the Talmud was written down and published. Beyond those two central works, there are many other important books that help us as Jews, but I would not call them the Word of God, like I would the Talmud and the Tanakh."

"And what are these other books?"

"Commentaries by great rabbis. Most important would be those by Rashi, who lived during the eleventh century A.D. I should also mention Moses Maimonides, who lived during the twelfth century A.D. Beyond that, there is the *Shulkhan Arukh,* written in the middle of the 1500s. And, of course, I should mention the *Responsa* literature. These are answers to questions posed by Jews of various centuries regarding how to apply Judaism's ancient laws."

Sean responded, "But what I'm more interested in is whether in Judaism there has ever been another 'Sinai experience.' All the revelation and commentary literature that you've talked about is just the outflow of the Torah. Has there ever been a prophet who was so great that he rivaled Moses?"

"No, absolutely not."

"Well then, it seems to me that you're missing a great deal. In my system of belief, the Torah is a great work, but it was just the first in a series of divine revelations. It was never intended to be the centerpiece of the religion of God's people."

"And why not? There is only one God. So why would there need to be more than one Torah?"

"Because it is unlike God to give only one Torah."

"Now there's a statement that's going to need some support—preferably from the Torah itself," Shlomo answered.

" 'Thou shalt not respect persons,' according to Deuteronomy 16:19," Sean responded.

"And that has something to do with the issue before us?"

"Yes, of course. God hates it when people show favoritism because it is against his nature to favor one person over another. And since he hates favoritism, he would never favor one generation—or one race—over another. Now here's my point: we should expect the same kind of revelation from God in every generation because it is unlike God to play favorites.

"This is one of the main problems with Judaism: it's a religion that rests on too small of a base. The Law of Moses is insufficient as a foundation to support the one true religion. The Pentateuch was never intended to be the 'end all' of divine revelation. Its primary purpose is to point ahead to the person and work of the Messiah, Jesus. I think this is the reason that your religion has to keep adding on stuff to the Tanakh. After a while, you felt like you had to have something that made the Torah relevant in the A.D. centuries. So you came up with the Mishnah. But that didn't really do the trick, so you added the Gemara. But even that wasn't quite right, so in came the commentaries by the rabbis. Still, however, many questions were left unanswered, so you came up with the *Responsa* literature."

"Well," Shlomo jumped in, "this seems like a case of the pot calling the kettle black. *You* represent the religion that keeps coming up with new revelations. Unlike other Christians, you don't think that the New Testament is enough. You had to add the Book of Mormon, which is subtitled 'Another Testament of Jesus Christ.' Then there's the *Doctrine and Covenants,* and the *Pearl of Great Price,* and the list goes on and on. And *then*—please correct me if I'm wrong—you believe that your apostles (the current leaders of your church) continue to have the authority to give new revelations!"

"Yes, well, that's my point. The truth is too big, too expansive, to be contained in a single book of revelations—or even several for that matter. If we are to know God's mind in every age, we must have revelation from him in every age."

"Sean, I think your problem is that you underestimate the power of a book that is truly divine." As Shlomo said this, he stood up to address Sean. "Because the Torah comes from God, it is sufficient for all time."

"Then why did you need to add to it? Why did you need more than the Tanakh?" Now Sean was standing.

"I've already covered this, but I can do it again. The Talmud is not new. It was there all along in oral form. It's just that it got written down after the Tanakh was completed."

"And what about the other stuff?" Sean was getting an edge in his voice.

"They are merely clarifications, not divine revelation."

"Well, that's what you say, but I know for a fact that that's not how you think. I can tell that—"

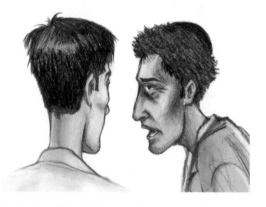

"Oh, so you can read my mind, eh, Sean?"

"Well, no. But I can see—"

"Gentlemen!" Jim broke in. "And I do use that term with some reservation. Please remember that we are not here to get angry with each other but to help our Sucher understand these five religions. Now, Fachmann Shlomo, you may respond to Sean, but you must do so with the civility that your venerable religion is well known for."

"I don't think I need to say anything else." With that, Shlomo sat down. Sean did too.

"OK," Jim said. "Sucher, who's next?"

"Javier."

Javier wasted no time. "What is the English translation of *Yom Kippur?*"

Shlomo looked surprised. "Day of Atonement."

"I want you to explain what the atonement is all about."

"Of course. *Yom Kippur* is the most solemn day in Judaism. It is a day for reflecting and repenting of our sins before the Judge of the universe, so that we are AT-ONE with God again. It is one of the many continuing witnesses to Judaism's enduring nature."

Javier was shaking his head. "I disagree. Does the Day of Atonement in modern times look anything like the Day of Atonement found in your Tanakh?"

"We no longer have the temple," Shlomo explained.

"That's not my problem," Javier said. "My Old Testament says, 'it is the blood that makes atonement.' What happened to the blood in your religion?"

"Since the temple was destroyed, the rabbis have said that our prayers

Old Testament sacrifices were a picture of Christ's ultimate sacrifice.

and our repentance can replace the temple sacrifice. The Day of Atonement is about afflicting one's soul, really. God honors our efforts as much as those efforts' results."

Sean guffawed. "Sounds like 'mere clarifications' to me." Shlomo glared at him.

"My good Fachmänner," Jim interrupted, "when Javier called for blood, he didn't mean yours. Sean, enough. Javier, Shlomo, please continue."

"I think Sean's jab just now was pretty perceptive," Javier said. "No amount of rabbinical reinterpretation can escape the fact that the Old Testament—pardon, the Tanakh—keeps to the principle of life for life. On what grounds do you base your atonement today?"

"God's mercy, of course."

"But what about Adam's sin? You cannot deny that you have been affected by Adam's sin. How can God be just to overlook it?" Javier demanded.

"First, I reject this Christian idea of 'original sin'—or whatever Jehovah's Witnesses call it. We pray that God's mercy will overcome His righteous wrath. The Talmud says that God prays to Himself that His mercy will overcome His justice. This is because He does not enjoy watching the wicked die; He is primarily merciful."

Javier shook his head. "Then your God wants to be *unjust.* Think about it, Shlomo: for God to be truly good, God's mercy must be just too. And there is no way for that to happen without an atonement. If you deny the atonement of Jesus Christ, you must deny either that God is a God of absolute justice or that there is such a thing as divine mercy or that sin is really sin. There's no way around it. Without the atonement, your religion is theologically shipwrecked." Javier paused. "I'm done."

God's mercy must be just too.
~Javier

Silently, we all waited, watching Shlomo. Finally, he said, "I don't see it that way, Javier. It should be obvious to all of us that God *wants* to have mercy on us."

"Donald," I said, "I think it's your turn now."

"Sean and Javier have been a perfect prologue to what I'm going to address," Donald began. "Sean, you observed that the Tanakh is incomplete without further revelation. Javier, you've pointed out that Judaism seems to have lost the idea of atonement. Now, Sucher, where do both these roads lead?"

Though I thought I knew, I still hesitated. "Well, Jesus Christ, I suppose. Christ is our sacrifice, right?"

"Yes, indeed," Donald responded, "and the main point that I want to drive home tonight is this: by rejecting Jesus of Nazareth as the Messiah, Judaism has become a religion that cannot make sense of itself."

Jim jumped in, with a shocked sort of laugh. "Wow, that's quite a charge, Donald. I don't think you're going to be able to make that one stick."

"Well, Donald," Shlomo added sarcastically, "please tell me how it is that I misunderstand my own religion."

Making Sense of Judaism

I. Judaism cannot make sense of the tabernacle and the temple.
II. Judaism cannot make sense of its own feasts.
III. Judaism cannot make sense of the Tanakh's emphasis on the Messiah.
IV. Judaism cannot make sense of the historical Jesus.

"I will use one of your own statements as a springboard. Before our break you said something like this: As Jews we believe that we can pray to God directly without a mediator. We do not need someone else to pray for us, live for us, or die for us."

"Yes, that sounds pretty close to what I said."

"Well, it doesn't sound like the Torah. When the Israelites made a covenant with God, God told them that they could not come near the mountain where His glory was being manifested."

"But before long," Shlomo said, "He was showing His people how they could approach Him."

"And how could they approach Him? It was not directly. God commanded Moses to have a tabernacle built. And I consider this to be the first way in which Judaism is not able to understand itself. Central to Jewish theology and history are the tabernacle and the temple. And yet when we examine these structures, we learn that through their furniture and their many rites, they stood as testimonies of the great distance between God and man. Man is sinful; God is holy. Man must have a holy, divinely appointed mediator to represent him before God. In the Torah, Aaron and his sons are the mediators. But, of course, these men could not themselves heal the breach between God and man. You see, it—"

"And why not?" Shlomo interrupted, his arms folded.

"Because those priests were themselves sinners and because the blood of animals cannot take away human sin. Nothing about Moses' tabernacle or Solomon's temple could reconcile man to God. Those rites simply *represented* the greater mediator who was to come. This idea is at the core of the New Testament book called *Hebrews*."

"Donald," Shlomo said, "let me remind you that I do not consider the author of Hebrews to be a credible source."

"But I am sure that you consider the Tanakh to be a credible source, and it is the Tanakh that the author of Hebrews uses to make his point. Consider these verses from Hebrews 10. I'll read it in English from my Greek New Testament."

HEBREWS 10

The blood of bulls and goats cannot take away sins. For this reason, when He [that is, the Messiah] came into the world, He said, "You [that is, God] have not desired sacrifice and offering. But You have prepared a body for me. . . . Then I [the Messiah] said, 'Behold, I come to do Your will, O God (in the scroll of the Book it is written about me).' " He [again, the Messiah] said first, "Sacrifice and offering . . . You have not desired." . . . Then He said, "Behold, I come to do Your will." Thus, He [that is, God] takes away the first in order to establish the second. And it is by this "will" that we have been sanctified, through the offering of the body of Jesus Christ once and for all.

PSALM 40th

"OK, I'm confused," I said.

"Sucher," Donald said, "the author of Hebrews is arguing for the necessity of embracing Jesus as the Messiah by citing Psalm 40:6–8, a passage that many Jews through the centuries have accepted as messianic. By quoting this psalm written by David, the author of Hebrews demonstrates that God never intended for sacrifices and offerings to take away sin; God has never desired sacrifice and offering. Those sacrifices served a higher purpose. They foreshadowed the coming of One who would do for God's people what the sacrificial animals never could do."

"Donald, there's no way you are going to convince me that David in Psalm 40 was talking about Jesus of Nazareth," Shlomo said, shaking his head.

"I don't have to; that's not my point. I'm simply showing that your view of the tabernacle is different from the Tanakh's. You say that Judaism teaches that mankind does not need a mediator. I'm saying that the Tanakh's presentation of the rites and structure of the tabernacle reveals that man must have a mediator. You also claim that the rites of the tabernacle were not picture prophecies—that they were simply God's way of keeping His people right with Him. But I'm saying that, according to Psalm 40, God never intended for the tabernacle's ceremonies to make His people righteous. Those rites simply pointed to someone about whom 'the scroll of the Book' was written—someone whose body was prepared by God for the purpose of doing what the sacrifices never could."

"And that someone is, of course, your Jesus," Shlomo said with a sarcastic chuckle.

"You can laugh all you want to, Shlomo, but the fact remains that my religion can account for the Tanakh's handling of the tabernacle and its ceremonies, whereas your religion cannot."

"Well, what else am I not able to understand?" Shlomo asked.

"Without accepting Jesus as the Messiah, you are not able to make good sense of the feasts of Judaism. Let me ask you, Shlomo: Why were these feasts so important?"

"Because God said they were important. Repeatedly in the Torah, the Lord tells His people to keep these feasts. And let me remind you that God's purpose for their observing these feasts is historical, not prophetic. For example, they were to keep the Passover so that they would never forget that God redeemed them from Egypt."

"OK, let's talk about the Passover," Donald continued. "Why is there so much emphasis on the Passover lamb? It must be flawless. Its blood must be shed in just the right way. That blood must then be applied to each person's house. The lamb must then be eaten according to strict specifications."

"Because that's what God said. God chose to protect His people from the death angel by the death of a lamb. We continue to observe the Passover because that is God's ordained means of reminding us of our deliverance from the oppressor."

"But *why* did He choose to deliver His people in that way?"

"I don't know. He just did. That's the problem with you Christians—you read messianic significance into everything."

"So, Shlomo, the answer is 'that's just how it is.' I think I have a more satisfying answer—one that relates to your inability to answer Javier's question about the atonement. I believe God chose

to deliver His people from Egypt by the blood of a lamb in order to foreshadow the coming Lamb of God. This idea is at the core of John's Gospel. In John 1:29, John the Baptist introduces Jesus as the ultimate Passover Lamb: 'Behold the Lamb of God, which taketh away the sin of the world.' And later when Jesus dies, it is during the time of the Passover feast. While Jews all over Jerusalem were killing their Passover lambs, Jesus was shedding His blood on a Roman cross so that God's people could be truly free—free from the oppression of sin."

Some of the items used in a Passover celebration

"I don't consider either John the Baptist or John the Apostle to have been a good Jew," Shlomo answered with a smile. "Like all Christians, they were way too messianic in their theology."

"I think we'll find that they were more in agreement with the Tanakh than modern-day Judaism is. And this brings me to consider the third way in which I believe your religion can't make sense of itself. Your view of the importance of the Messiah (or unimportance, I should say) disagrees with the Tanakh and with much of your own history. It is disturbing to me how the Messiah is downplayed today in your religion."

"He's not. Well, as I said before, we can't speculate. If God hasn't said much about something, neither can we."

"Hasn't said much about the *Messiah?!* How can you read the Neviim without being acutely aware of the fact that a great descendant of David is coming to deliver His people not just from their enemies but also from *themselves?* The history of Judaism testifies to the validity of the point I'm making. For most of your people's history, there has been a strong messianic expectation. But in the last few centuries, you have become disillusioned with the Messiah. Judaism no longer anticipates the great Deliverer who is anticipated everywhere in the Tanakh."

"There is a reason for that, Donald. We have learned that it is irresponsible for us to just sit around and wait for the Messiah to come and deliver us. The Messiah will come one day. Until then, however, we must work to deliver ourselves."

"That is, perhaps, one of the most condemning confessions you can make as a Jew. It shows that you are out of step with the Tanakh. This is the reason I am very comfortable saying that the Christian Scriptures are a much better complement to the Tanakh than Judaism is. The Tanakh everywhere anticipates that the Messiah is coming, and the New Testament everywhere proclaims that the Messiah has come."

"I refuse to accept as Messiah a man who died a humiliating death on a Roman cross," Shlomo said with emotion. "This is not the Messiah spoken of in the Tanakh. You want me to accept a Messiah who was humiliated and killed by the Gentiles. Through the centuries the Gentiles have tried to take away from us every-thing we hold dear. And now you are asking me to accept your belief that the Gentiles took away our Messiah too? Ridiculous!"

"Shlomo, then what will you do with this Jesus of Nazareth? This is the fourth and final way in which I believe Judaism is not able to understand itself. You are not able to account for the histor-ical Jesus in a way that is consis-tent with your Judaism. The godly example of Jesus of Nazareth is very attractive to you. You yourself have said that Jesus was a good man. But you deny both His deity

> *If Jesus had not been the Messiah, He could not have been a good man.*
> ~Donald

and His messianic calling. Thus, your judgment of Jesus is hope-lessly conflicted. If Jesus had not been the Messiah, He could not have been a good man. Jesus claimed to be the Messiah and taught that God is His Father. He said that all people are obligated to honor Him just as they honor His Father. A good man does not make such claims—*unless those claims are true!*"

"No, I disagree," Shlomo quickly responded. "It is possible for a good person to be confused about such matters."

"So Jesus was a lunatic?"

"Well, I wouldn't call Jesus a lunatic—just a little confused."

"A little confused? So if I stood up and announced sincerely and emphatically that I was the Son of God, you would say that I was just 'a little confused'? Shlomo, to borrow a thought from C. S. Lewis, I tell you that the Bible requires that you make one of three judgments regarding this Jesus: either Jesus was a liar, or He was a lunatic, or He was who He claimed to be—*the Lord.*"

"Jesus is not Lord!"

"Then what is He?"

"I don't know. All religions at some point have their mysteries. This is, I guess, one of mine. Some of my Orthodox brothers are comfortable calling your Jesus a liar. I, however, am not. I recognize that their position is more consistent than mine, but that doesn't mean that my position is impossible."

"But, Shlomo, it does mean that on this point your religion does not understand itself."

"Well, that's *your* claim."

"It is indeed," Donald said with a satisfied smile.

"Shlomo," Jim interrupted, "it's getting late. Can you wrap up tonight's Auseinandersetzung?"

"Certainly," Shlomo said. "Sucher, I can respond to everything that Donald has said tonight by pointing out that he has not proved that his Jesus is the Messiah. All he's done is show that his religion fits *his reading* of the Tanakh. But, you see, the Tanakh is not a Christian book; it is a Jewish book. So it's not his reading that matters. It's my reading that matters, and my reading of the Tanakh supports my religion much better than it supports Christianity."

Just a Prophet

3

While we were leaving, Jim got all of us to commit to coming back the next night, a Tuesday, for Hamid's presentation. Since Christianity is chronologically next in the history of religions, we were supposed to hear from Donald. But I told Jim that I wanted to hear him last.

As Tuesday morning became Tuesday afternoon, I was surprised at how I felt about the coming Auseinandersetzung. I wasn't dreading it; I was looking forward to it. I had been nervous before because I thought I was going to look stupid or uninformed. But what I kept realizing during the presentation and refutation of Shlomo's views was that the things I don't understand are things that many people don't; and when I asked the questions that naturally came to my mind, I got good, helpful answers. So I guess what I'm saying is, debate is fun, and I hope that my life is filled with many more "Auseinandersetzungs"—of one sort or another.

"Since we're all here, let's go ahead and start," Jim began.

I noticed that the room was a little different. Jim, or maybe it was Jenny, had brought in another armchair—I guess so that the "loveseat mess" wouldn't get repeated. Too bad. I thought it added a cool dimension to the interaction.

Islam is a religion of peace, equality, and true freedom.
~Hamid

"Thank you for this great privilege and opportunity." Hamid was sitting alone in the loveseat. He looked comfortable and very calm. "I must begin this presentation by assuring you, my Sucher, that Islam is badly misunderstood in America. Islam is a religion of peace, equality, and true freedom."

Involuntarily—and much to my embarrassment—a grin crept across my face.

"Something is funny, Sucher?"

"No, it's nothing at all."

"Only the mentally ill smile at nothing."

"Well, I don't mean to be unkind, Hamid, but everything I know about Islam contradicts what you just said."

"That is because everything you know about Islam is not very much at all. You should trust my perspective; it is one of the best-informed perspectives you will ever be able to hear." Believe it or not, when Hamid said that, he didn't sound arrogant at all—just matter-of-fact.

"Well then, you've got a lot of explaining to do," Jenny jumped in. "What you're saying sounds good in a historical vacuum, but recent events make your claim very difficult to support." It's nice to have her around. She feels free to ask the questions I don't have the nerve to ask.

"Recent events are recent. Islam, however, is ancient. Its story begins with the remarkable life of a good and sincere man who was born around A.D. 570. Muhammad, of the tribe of Quraysh, was born in the very important Arabian city of Mecca. Hardship was a way

of life for him from the beginning. His father died before he was born. His uncle raised him, training him to excel as a merchant in the Quraysh tribe. In his travels Muhammad learned much about people and religion, for his trade carried him throughout Arabia and into Syria. Eventually, he gained the confidence of Khadijah, a wealthy widow of Mecca, journeying in her service for some time. His disciplined way of life gained more than her profes-sional confidence, however, for eventually they married. This mar-riage (to a woman fifteen years his senior) gave Muhammad a power and prestige in Mecca that his future calling would need.

"Now, a word about Mecca. It was a very important center for trade in the Arabian Peninsula, and for many years before Muhammad's birth it had been considered a holy city. In this city was the sacred *Kaaba,* which is Arabic for 'cube.' This small,

A close-up photo of the Kaaba

cube-shaped shrine was believed to have been erected by Abraham and his son Ishmael for the worship of Allah, the one true God.

"But the Meccans' understanding of Allah had been terribly twisted by many centuries of pagan Arabian influences. By the time Muhammad was born, the Meccans were idolaters. They had filled the Kaaba with images that they claimed were 'daughters of Allah.' Every year, Arabs from all over would journey to pay homage to the Kaaba and its grievous idols."

"So Muhammad was an idolater too, I guess?" I asked.

"No, no, no. Muhammad was a good and perceptive man. He was made of firmer stuff than could be easily conformed to pagan culture. He knew that the Kaaba worship was wrong, and he would often pray and meditate, searching for Allah to reveal himself. Eventually, he was able to spend an entire month out of every year in such meditations, the month of Ramadan. In the year 610, during one of these times of seclusion, Muhammad received his first revelation. He was in a trance and heard a terrifying voice say, 'Read!' But he insisted that he could not, for he was illiterate. But the voice insisted that he was chosen to read for Allah. When he awoke, he left the cave where he was and went out to the hillside. Then a glorious being appeared to him and announced: 'O Muhammad! You are Allah's messenger, and I am Gabriel.'

"Contrary to what some suppose, Muhammad was not at all pleased by this revelation. He told Khadijah that he feared he was being accosted by evil spirits. But his wife wisely assured him that Allah would not allow a harmful spirit to deceive such an honest and good man as he. After much soul-searching, he became convinced that it was indeed Gabriel and that Allah was calling him to be his special prophet to the Arab peoples.

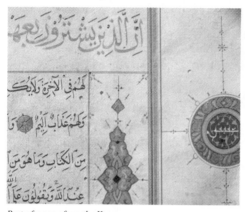
Part of a page from the Koran

"Over the next twenty years, Muhammad received one revelation after another, each while he was in the state of a trance. Shortly after the prophet's death, these revelations were compiled into a single volume called the *Koran*. This is an Arabic word meaning 'reading' or 'recitation,' based on Muhammad's first command from Gabriel: 'Read!'

"These revelations were the basis for Muhammad's preaching. By 613, Muhammad was proclaiming Allah's message all over Mecca."

"Let me guess," Jenny said. "The Meccans didn't like what Muhammad had to say."

"That would be an understatement," Hamid continued. "Muhammad's own Quraysh tribe, which dominated Mecca's social and political life, became actively hostile. Muhammad's preaching was gaining a number of converts, who turned from idolatry and polytheism. Then they stopped venerating the Kaaba (because of the idolatry associated with it), which hurt the income of the wealthy Meccans, who profited greatly from the commerce that the Kaaba brought to Mecca.

"But persecution cannot quench truth, and the numbers of converts (who came to be called Muslims) grew and grew—and not just in Mecca. A group of travelers from Medina heard Muhammad preach and believed that he was the prophet about whom they had heard many predictions. In Medina there were many learned Jews who had often told the pagans of a great prophet to come who would arise out of Arabia and rid the Arabs of their paganism. These men embraced Muhammad's teachings and returned to Medina, where they quickly saw Muslim belief saturate the city. Soon afterwards, officials from Medina traveled to Mecca— a distance of about two hundred miles—to invite Muhammad to live in their city.

"Once news of Muhammad's possible move reached the Quraysh leaders in Mecca, they were very disturbed. Since Muhammad had become influential while being persecuted, what would happen if he were allowed to live in Medina unopposed? They began to plot Muhammad's murder. But Allah is wiser than man. He gave his prophet two revelations that he would need to survive the coming fierce opposition. First, he told him that it would soon be time to fight for the truth of Allah, 'until persecution is no more and religion is for Allah only.' Second, he told him to leave for Medina.

"Muhammad's flight from Mecca to Medina was a watershed event in the history of Islam—indeed, in the history of the world. We call it the *Hijrah*, which is Arabic for 'flight.' It took place on June 20, 622. From that central event, Muslims the world over date all events, just as Christians do with the birth of Jesus. The thirteen years of humiliation were over. Now, at last, the Muslim era had begun. In the next ten years, the last in Muhammad's earthly life, Islam would go from being the faith of a few to being the dominant religion of the Arabian Peninsula.

> *Muhammad's flight from Mecca to Medina was a watershed event in the history of Islam—indeed, in the history of the world. We call it the* Hijrah.
> ~Hamid

"But let me hasten to add that Muhammad and the Muslims faced many difficult challenges. The first challenge came from those who were supposed to be Muhammad's followers, the Jews and the Hypocrites. When the prophet first came to Medina, the Jews welcomed him. But when they learned that he had not come to give them dominion over Arabia but to make them fellow believers with all the Arabs who submitted to Islam, they were appalled. Therefore, they spoke out against him and tried to dissuade him from his mission. Some Arabs were convinced by these Jews, and they secretly sought to defeat the prophet. These are known in the Koran as 'the Hypocrites.'

"One cause of strife was the issue of the *Qiblah*. The Qiblah was the place that Muslims were to face in prayer. Up to this time, it had been Jerusalem. But early in Muhammad's career in

The Dome of the Rock, located on Jerusalem's temple mount, stands over one of the holiest sites in Islam. It was here, say the Muslims, that Abraham attempted to offer Ishmael, and it was from this spot that Muhammad is said to have been caught up into heaven.

Medina, he received a revelation indicating that all Muslims were now to face the Kaaba when they prayed. The Jews took offense at this, thinking that Muhammad favored his own people above them. In truth, he was simply following Allah's orders."

"OK, wait a minute," I said. "Why were Muslims facing Jerusalem in prayer in the first place? Except for Abraham, Islam and Judaism don't have anything in common, right?"

"No, that's not true. Through Allah's many revelations, Muhammad learned that he was Allah's last prophet. Most of the previous prophets were men of renown in Judaism. Abraham, Moses, David—these were all considered to be messengers of Allah, and at the beginning of Muhammad's ministry, he was convinced that the Jews were Allah's special people."

The name Allah, shown here in Arabic, is one of the most common elements in Muslim visual art.

"But the Jews have never served Allah. You'll never find the name *Allah* in the Old Testament."

"The word *Allah* is simply the Arabic word for 'God.' In the West people take the word to refer to the God of Islam, but in Arabic *Allah* is simply *God*.

"But now I want to turn your attention to Muhammad's greater opposition, the Quraysh tribe. He knew that unless he dealt with them decisively, they would in time attack Medina and destroy Islam. Since Allah had already told him to fight for the faith, he set about to find a way to defeat the Quraysh.

"His opportunity came in the second year of the Hijrah. A Meccan merchants' caravan from Syria was returning to Mecca and was passing by close to Medina. Muhammad led his Muslims to attack the Meccans. But they escaped him, returned to Mecca, and then went back out to meet his forces at a place called Badr. Muhammad seemed to be hopelessly outnumbered, but the great Battle of Badr proved to be a signal victory for the Muslims. The fame of Muhammad and his faith quickly traveled all over Arabia, and those who had opposed him in Medina, the Jews and the Hypocrites, lost power and influence.

"There were still many difficult struggles ahead, which I do not have the time to detail for you. What is important for you to remember is the truly decisive moment that came in 630. It was then that Muhammad marched on Mecca with ten thousand troops. His old Quraysh opponents from previous conflicts did not even attempt to fight. Mecca received her once-hated son with open arms. It was an act of Allah. All Meccans became Muslims, the Kaaba was purged of its idols, and Mecca became the holy city of Islam."

"And that's the story of Islam?" I asked.

"Well, that is Muhammad's story. He died in 632, the undisputed master of Arabia. Allah had used him to bring true religion to the benighted, pagan tribes of the Arabian Peninsula. He brought it by giving the people the Koran, the very words of Allah.

"I should give you some information that will help you, Sucher, understand how we got from 632 to today. Shortly after Muhammad's death, his closest friends selected Abu Bakr (his most trusted advisor) to serve as the *caliph,* the leader of the Islamic state. During the reigns of the first four caliphs (from 632 to 661) Islam spread from Arabia to Palestine, Syria, Persia, Egypt, and Libya. The first four caliphs were careful to be fair to all faiths. Jews and Christians were not persecuted; they were permitted to retain their respective beliefs. These caliphs even permitted them to enjoy influential positions in society.

"From 661 to 750 the caliphate was under the control of the Umayyad Dynasty, who moved the empire's capital from Medina to Damascus. By the early 700s, Islam covered all of North Africa and all of Spain. But the Umayyads, becoming drunk with power, allowed only Arabs into the ruling class, and everyone else—

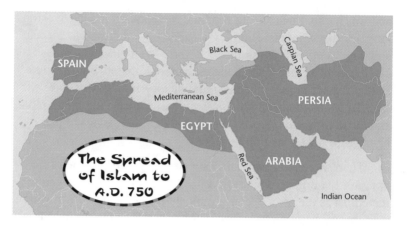

The Spread of Islam to A.D. 750

whether Muslim or not—was reduced to a second-class status. Resentment grew throughout the empire, for the majority of the citizens were non-Arabic.

"Civil war broke out in the mid-700s, and when the smoke cleared, the Muslim world was ruled by the Abbasid Dynasty from 750 to 1258. The center of their government was Baghdad, near the cradle of the world's earliest civilizations. The Abbasids' rule was marked by great achievements in high culture, economic prosperity, good education, and extensive trade. The Abbasids failed, however, to unite the world of Islam. Not long after 750,

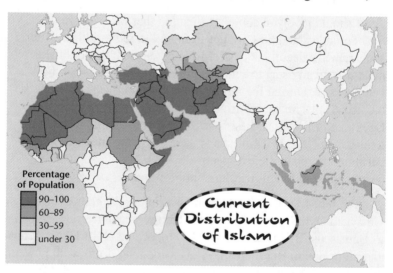

Percentage of Population

- 90–100
- 60–89
- 30–59
- under 30

Current Distribution of Islam

the Muslims in Spain broke away from Baghdad and formed their own caliphate. In time the same happened in North Africa and in Persia. But this was not the failure of Islam. It was only the failure of men to unite this one faith under one government. Allah knows best. He knew that the one true faith could be spread more efficiently by many different Islamic states than by one huge empire.

"And so it has. Today Islam dominates an almost solid line of nations from Morocco in the west to Indonesia in the east, and it claims more than one billion adherents in almost every country on the globe. And—let me hasten to add—the vast majority of them are not of Arab descent. Islam is not the religion of the Arabs. It is the religion of Allah, and it is for *the world.*"

"Let me remind you, Hamid," Jim said, "that if you're going to have time to cover Muslim beliefs and to get in some meaningful cross-examination, you'll need to end this historical survey soon."

"Do not worry, Jim. I am right on schedule. Let me now begin my presentation of Muslim doctrine and practice by saying that what I am about to do will just barely scratch the surface of all that Muslims believe. Although Islam is a very unified and simple religion, there are many differences of opinion among Muslims. There are Sunnis, Shiites, and Sufis. But my concern is to show you what is central. First, I will discuss the foundations of Islam. Second, Islam's basic beliefs. And third, we will consider the famous Five Pillars of Islam.

"To every Muslim, there are two key sources of authority. The first is the Koran, which records the many revelations that Muhammad received from 610 until his death in 632. Organized into 114 chapters called *surahs,* it is roughly the size of the Christian's New Testament. The Koran was revealed in Arabic, and

---

GET THE BIG PICTURE

The Doctrine and Practice of the Muslims

I. Foundations of Islam
II. Basic Beliefs of Islam
III. Five Pillars of Islam

though I am glad that the words of the Koran have been rendered in other languages, you must understand that what results is *not* the Koran. This is important for you to note, Sucher, because I have often heard non-Muslims who do not know Arabic criticize what they think is the Koran. To them I reply, 'If you have not read the words of Allah in Arabic, you have not read the words of Allah.'

"Now, let me mention the second source of authority for Islam. The Koran addresses many things, but not everything that Muslims need to know is in the Koran. Therefore, Allah has given us the *Hadith,* which means 'report,' a collection of the words and deeds of the prophet. By seeking to pattern every part of our lives (as individuals and as a society) after the life of Muhammad, Muslims

A Muslim praying in India

please Allah. You may wish to think of the Koran as the words of Allah and the Hadith as Allah's ordained application of his words to various situations.

"From these two authorities, the Koran and the Hadith, Muslims derive the basic doctrines of their faith. As a sort of introduction to these basic beliefs, let me mention two ideas that are foundational even to these basic beliefs. The first is the word *Islam* itself. This is the Arabic word meaning 'submission.' The word *Muslim* is related to it; it means 'one who is submitted.' At its core, my religion is simply submission to Allah's will.

"Now, I must hasten to add that although this idea of submission is fundamental to Islam, it is, of course, meaningless until the will of Allah is defined. What makes Islam's concept of submission to the divine will unique is the *shahadah,* which means 'witness' or 'testimony.' This is the great confession of Islam: *La ilaha ill Allah, Muhammad rasul Allah*—'There is no God but Allah; Muhammad is the messenger of Allah.' To say these words with sincerity is to convert to Islam, for believing this brief creed with all one's heart is submission to Allah. Let me now briefly outline what this means for Islamic doctrine.

"First, we must realize that it has profound implications for our understanding of Allah. Allah is one and unique. Thus, at the heart of Islam is a firm commitment to rejecting Christianity's doctrine of the Trinity. The Trinity defies the whole idea of Islam. My religion is all about mankind's submission to Allah. But fundamental to Christianity's doctrine is this idea that there is a man who is *not submitted* to Allah but is said to be *equal* with Allah. Pride is the cardinal sin in Islam because pride is a flouting of the submission that Allah requires of everyone. By saying that Jesus of Nazareth is God Himself, Christians attempt to make this very good man guilty of a most egregious pride—ascribing to oneself partnership with Allah. For this reason the Koran clearly states in Surah 4:171: 'Believe in Allah and His messengers, and say not "Three"—Cease! It is better for you!—Allah is only One God. Far is it removed from His transcendent majesty that He should have a son.' "

"Whew!" Jenny said, looking over at me. "It's easy to understand that one, eh Steve?" I nodded.

"But there is much more to Islam's conception of Allah than its rejection of the Trinity," Hamid went on to say. "I should also mention some of Allah's characteristics. The Koran teaches that Allah is the creator and sustainer of all things, and all things work together to accomplish his perfect will. As the only completely sovereign being in the universe, he is also the judge of his creatures. He can be trusted to judge all because he is completely just, righteous, and good.

"Now when I say that Allah is just and will judge all flesh, many people conclude that he is therefore cruel and uncaring. This is a terrible misrepresentation of Allah. Over and over again we read in the Koran the words, 'Lo! Allah is Forgiving, Merciful.' This is seen in the fact that he delights to guide all his creatures who choose to follow him. It does not matter what they may have done or what their nationality may be. Allah is not the God of the perfect, nor is he the God of the Arabs only. He is the God of all who will confess with sincerity the shahadah.

"I will now present Islam's understanding of man. The Genesis account of the creation of man and woman is accepted by the

Man Koran, with a few differences. Muslims believe that Adam sinned against Allah and therefore fell from the perfection in which he had been made. However, the Koran denies the Christian concept of original sin. The Koran teaches that Allah forgave Adam and restored him to his original position as his most exalted creation."

"So mankind is without sin—perfect?" I knew Hamid would say no. But I thought it was a question that needed to be asked.

"No." See. "Everything in the universe, except for Allah, is limited. Mankind's limitation is that he tends to be rebellious and proud. He is frail when it comes to temptations to be self-sufficient. He longs to make himself a partner with Allah. This is the reason that Muhammad emphasized that the true religion is *Islam* ('submission')."

"OK, now let me get this straight," I said. "Allah made man. Man sinned. Allah forgave man, but man is frail and easily tempted to be proud. So how does a person get to heaven?"

"He repents. And he 'submits' to Allah in pledging complete allegiance to his maker, by confessing the shahadah with all his heart. When a person sincerely embraces this truth, he is then restored to the state of sinlessness in which he was born.

Prophecy "Now, let me move on, Sucher, to mention what Muslims believe about prophecy (or divine revelation, as some may call it) and about the coming Day of Judgment. Both of these are very important to Islam's system of belief.

"Without prophets who faithfully speak for Allah, the human race is left on the tumultuous sea of life without a rudder or a compass. Some suppose that Islam believes in only one prophet, Muhammad. But we recognize many prophets throughout the history of the world. The first was Adam. After him came many holy men that are familiar to everyone in this room: Noah, Abraham, Moses, Jonah, Job, and Jesus (to name a few)."

"OK, now I'm really confused," and I was too. "You oppose Christianity and Judaism, but you think that the founders of both religions were right—that they were God's prophets?"

"Muhammad is the last of Allah's prophets. Allah called him not only to reveal new advances in the progress of his revelation but also to correct what had been corrupted in the earlier prophecies. Moses wrote the Torah, and it was true. Jesus authorized the writing of the Gospels, and they were true. However, shortly after these revelations were completed, wicked men corrupted them. Through Muhammad—in the Koran and the Hadith—Allah set straight what had become crooked."

"Then let me ask you this, Hamid," Jenny began. "What was wrong in the Torah and the Gospels that had to be corrected?"

"Concerning the Torah, Muhammad revealed that the focus on the Jews as God's chosen people was a corruption. I think one example will suffice. Muhammad taught that the story of the sacrifice of Isaac in Genesis had been twisted by Jews who wanted people to think that Allah had special regard for Isaac and his descendants. Muhammad revealed that Abraham did not attempt to sacrifice Isaac but rather Ishmael."

"And the Gospels?" she asked.

"Well, I have already mentioned one corruption. Christians tampered with the text until it appeared to teach that Jesus was Allah's son who came to earth to die for the sins of humanity. I do believe that Jesus was a great prophet. The Koran teaches that Jesus was born of a virgin and performed many miracles. But it denies that Jesus came to die on the cross for sin. Since Allah always honors his prophets, it is inconceivable that Jesus should have actually died there. After being taken down from the cross, Jesus revived. Allah delivered this great prophet from death not by resurrection. He kept Jesus from dying in the first place.

"Let us now talk about the Day of Judgment. Over one quarter of the Koran's verses speak of the end. A day of doom is coming in which all living

Day of Judgment

will die and will be resurrected to stand before the heavenly throne. The deeds of all will be judged by Allah's Book of Deeds. Those whose good deeds are greater than their evil deeds will go to paradise, a garden of eternal pleasure. Those whose deeds have been primarily evil will be thrown into hellfire.

"Now, I should hasten to add that for many who go there, it is only temporary. Hell is a place of purging. As soon as a person has been purged of his evil deeds, his good deeds allow him to be taken to heaven. For those who have no good works to their credit, hell will be their lot forever."

"So how does one do good and thus come to deserve heaven?" That was Jenny's question.

"You must follow the Straight Path that the Koran shows. It basically involves a firm commitment to five duties, known to most as the Five Pillars of Islam.

Shahadah

"The first one we have already discussed—the shahadah. One cannot begin to please Allah unless he sincerely embraces Allah as the only God and Muhammad as his chosen prophet. Because this confession of faith is so important, Muslims quote it regularly, both publicly and privately.

Salat

"Second, I should mention *salat,* or 'prayers.' Every believer in Allah is to pray five times daily: before sunrise, at noon, in the afternoon, immediately after sunset, then just before going to bed. These prayers are to be done according to an established ritual that involves bowing several times toward the holy Kaaba in Mecca and reciting certain prescribed words. These prayers are special on Friday, which is the holy day in Islam. On that day Muslims gather to pray at the nearest *masjid* (or *mosque,* as many in the West call it). There the *imam* (the one who leads the congregation in prayer) recites verses from the Koran and delivers a sermon based on those verses.

Muslims are called to prayer at the mosque from chanting performed from the minaret.

"The third pillar is the *zakat,* which means 'purification.' This is a tax that the devout pay in order to help the poor and needy. The fourth pillar, *sawm,* involves fasting during the month of Ramadan."

Zakat

Sawm

"You don't eat for a month?!"

"Oh no. It is a fast that lasts only from sunrise to sunset. Once evening begins the Muslim is free to eat. And as the Koran suggests, we fast during this month to show our deep gratitude to Allah for giving us his revelations through the prophet.

"Now, let me mention the final pillar, the *hajj.* This is the pilgrimage to Mecca. Surah 2:196 says: 'Perform the pilgrimage and the visit to Mecca for Allah.' Every Muslim who is able to do so must travel to Mecca at least once. By traveling to Mecca, the pilgrim becomes intimately familiar with the people and events that are central to his faith. He sees where Muhammad grew up, he touches the Kaaba, and he is reminded that great sacrifice is often necessary to live for Allah."

Hajj

The Kaaba, a cube covered with black cloth, is in Mecca. Muslims pray toward it five times daily.

"And that's it— that's all there is to the Straight Path?"

"Yes, Sucher. I could give many more specifics, but this in brief is the way of Islam—the way of submission to Allah."

"OK then. What about me? I mean, do you think that I will go to heaven or hell? You've said that a person must follow the Straight Path to get to heaven, and you've outlined five duties that I've never done and that I never plan to do."

"This is a matter of some controversy in Islam. Some scholars would say that each person in the Day of Judgment will be judged according to his own beliefs, according to the holy books of his own religion. In that case—"

"And that's what you believe?"

"Well . . . uh . . . to answer you simply, I must say *no*. I cannot see how Allah could allow anyone into his heaven who does not even believe the shahadah."

"So I'm on my way to hell—forever?"

"Yes."

"What?!" Jim interrupted. "Hamid, you've never talked like this before."

"That is because, Jim, you have never asked me a question like that one before. Sucher, let me just say that remaining a Christian is a very dangerous thing. This is why I have chosen to participate in this Auseinandersetzung. Allah is willing to forgive all who will submit to him. So I urge you—all of you—to cry out with all sincerity: *La ilaha ill Allah, Muhammad rasul Allah!*"

"OK, Jim, that's it," I said. "I don't have any more questions."

As the Fachmänner started moving around for our break, I just kept thinking about Hamid's presentation. Evidently, I was doing nothing else.

"Steve," Jenny said, "are you OK?"

"What? Uh . . . yeah. I'm fine. Why?"

"Well, you're just staring blankly at the wall. That's why."

"Oh really? I hadn't noticed. You know, I think I'm going to take my break outside. I need some fresh air to get my brain back on track."

I quickly excused myself and walked out the front door. *Praise God for fall,* I thought to myself. The air was crisp, and bright yellow maple leaves were all over the ground. With my hands in my pockets,

I kicked a few leaves and looked up at the sky. *Stars, stars, stars. O God, they're beautiful.* In the starlight I could see my breath. "What is your life? It is even a vapour." *Only a vapor, God? I have so little time to get answers to life's most important questions.*

"God, how can I know that what I believe is right? I just don't understand!" There. I had said it—out loud even.

"What don't you understand?"

"Jenny, what are you doing out here?"

"Checking on you."

"I said I was OK, didn't I?"

"Yes, and I didn't believe you."

"Have you ever been wrong? No, wait. Don't answer that."

"I wasn't going to."

"I don't know, Jenny. It's just that while I was talking to Hamid, it hit me. It doesn't matter who you are, how good you've been, or how sincere you are about your beliefs—there's always someone (no, *millions* of someones, who are all smart and sincere) convinced you're going to hell!"

"But, Steve, it doesn't matter what the 'millions' believe about the world and about me. The only thing that really matters is what *God* knows to be true. If *He* approves of me, I'll be fine in this world and in the one to come."

"And how do you know that He approves?"

"If I trust Him, I am on His side. Nothing else matters."

"Well, Jenny, it's easy to say those things when you're at church, surrounded by people who all believe the same thing. It's a different story when you're talking with someone like Hamid or Shlomo or whoever—sincere people who are very smart."

"I spend more time every week with people like that than I do with people at church."

"Oh yeah, that's right. College life and Homer's aren't exactly havens for the tender Christian soul. Hmm."

"And I must admit that more than once I've asked myself the same questions you've just been asking. But I keep coming back to what Peter told Jesus when he was forced to confront unbelief: 'Lord, to whom shall we go? thou hast the words of eternal life. And we believe and are sure that thou art that Christ, the Son of the living God.' No one ever cared for me like Jesus. So why would I leave Him for someone (or something) else?"

"Hey, unless you two want to let Hamid off without a challenge, you'd better get back in here." Jim, of course.

Jenny and I went in and took our seats on the couch.

"All right, Sucher. Who'll be first?" Jim opened.

"Shlomo, I was wondering if you would like to question Hamid about Islam's reputation for violence," I offered.

"Yes indeed. Hamid, I thought it was almost humorous how you painted a whitewash of Islam's history and beliefs. You told our Sucher that the reason he thought Islam was violent was that he did not know much about it. Well, I assure you that I am not ignorant of your religion, but I do believe that Islam is a great danger to the world's well-being. And let me add that your attempt to cover up this fact was not only uncon- vincing, but it was also very damaging to your credibility."

"Well, my Jewish friend, please tell me what in particular was lacking from my presentation."

"*Jihad*—in a word. You never mentioned it. I find that incredible when you consider what an important role the concept of jihad has played in the history of Islam. In fact, many educated observers— Muslims among them—have concluded that jihad is the *sixth* Pillar of Islam."

"And what exactly is your concept of jihad?"

"Holy war against the 'infidels.' "

"Ah, yes. And there is our problem. *Jihad* does not mean 'holy war.' It refers to any struggle for Allah. Sending out missionaries, studying the Koran in school, seeking to conquer one's inner desires—each of these is a type of jihad."

> Jihad *does not mean 'holy war.' It refers to any struggle for Allah.*
> ~Hamid

"Killing Jews or Christians because they do not believe the way you do?" Shlomo asked right away. Whew! Things were definitely getting interesting again.

"The Koran does not allow Muslims to kill non-Muslims simply because they are not followers of Islam," Hamid answered.

"But the Koran does encourage Muslims to kill."

"Do you have a particular statement in mind, Shlomo?"

"I thought you'd never ask." Shlomo pulled out what must have been an English translation of the Koran. "Surah 9:29: 'Fight against such of those who have been given the Scripture as believe not in Allah nor the Last Day, and forbid not that which Allah hath forbidden by His messenger, and follow not the religion of truth, until they pay the tribute readily, being brought low.' It sounds to me as if 'those who have been given the Scripture' are Christians and Jews, right?"

"That is the Koran's normal designation for Jews and Christians," Hamid replied smoothly.

The fundamental importance of war in the spread of Islam is seen in the flag of Saudi Arabia. It combines two elements: the shahadah (written in Arabic) and a sword.

"So the Koran teaches that you're supposed to fight against people like me—and our Sucher here—until you've taken from us our ability to affect our cultures with our own beliefs!"

"You must attempt to understand the Koranic statement in its historical context. Allah was telling Muhammad about fighting people who wanted to destroy Islam. The statement is nothing more than a call to self-defense.

"Let me explain. A fundamental concept in Islam is the idea of the community, called the *ummah*. Repeatedly, the Koran exhorts the reader to sacrifice himself and his possessions for the sake of the well-being of the ummah. He is to do this in a number of ways. One common way is the zakat, as I mentioned before our break. By giving to the poor, the Muslim helps to sustain the Islamic community worldwide by meeting the needs of its weakest members. Of course, sometimes the ummah faces just as serious a threat from ideologies that refuse to recognize the legitimacy of Islam.

"Here I point you to Islam's first military conflicts. As I have mentioned, in the second year after the Hijrah, Muhammad led the Muslims to attack a Meccan merchants' caravan. It is true that those merchants posed no immediate threat to the Muslims."

"And yet," Shlomo jumped in, "he planned the attack anyway. Interesting! I hope you're listening, Sucher."

"As I was saying," Hamid continued, "the well-being of the ummah is very important. And those who devote themselves to harming it are to be punished—whether they are part of the community or not. These Meccans wanted to kill Muhammad and his followers. The fact that they were not attempting to do so on that particular day makes little difference in the mind of Allah. Just as the United States has been justified in ambushing its unsuspecting opponents in war, so also Muhammad was justified in attacking those Meccans that day."

"So it's OK to convert people at gunpoint," Shlomo retorted.

"No, the goal of Islamic war is not Islamic conversion. The goal is to punish those who seek to harm the ummah and to insure the ummah's future safety. Conversion by force is forbidden in Islam. So when Islam conquered Palestine, North Africa, and other lands shortly after the days of Muhammad, Christians and Jews were not forced to become Muslims. Politics, culture, and various forms of religious expression changed, naturally. But nobody *had* to become a Muslim."

The goal of Islamic war is not Islamic conversion. The goal is to . . . insure the ummah's future safety.
~Hamid

"Well," Shlomo said, "if understanding Surah 9:29 in context is so important, why don't you tell us just exactly what that verse's historical context was?"

"Surah 9 is generally believed to have been written in the ninth year after the Hijrah, which would be A.D. 631. That was the year that Muhammad organized a military campaign against Syria, which was a Christian land at the time. So I think that understanding this verse in its original context would mean seeing it as the justification for that military move."

"So why did Muhammad attack Syria?" I asked.

"Because the Syrians posed a threat to the well-being of the ummah in Mecca, Medina, and other places in Arabia. At that time Syria was officially Christian, and Syria felt something had to be done to stop the 'new religion' that was developing in Arabia."

"But Syria," Shlomo said, "is hundreds of miles from Mecca. What kind of threat are we talking about here?"

Medina is approximately two hundred miles from Mecca, while Syria is over eight hundred miles away.

"Armies can travel. Though they were many miles from Mecca, the Syrians could have invaded. In fact, Muhammad was confident that they were planning to do so."

"So what happened?" I asked.

"It ended peacefully. When the Muslims arrived at the border of Syria, they found that the Christian forces had not yet formed. Muhammad elected not to confront the Christians."

"But after Muhammad died, the Muslims did attack Syria, right?" I asked.

"Yes, that's right, Sucher."

"And then they attacked modern-day Israel, Iraq, Iran, Egypt, all of North Africa, and then Spain," Jenny added.

"I suppose that's one way to condense history."

"So what sort of threat did *Spain* pose to the Arabian ummah?"

"To Muslims in Arabia . . . none. But to those in North Africa . . . well, that's a different story."

"Oh, c'mon," Jenny almost snorted. "Do you really believe that Muslims invaded Spain, and then France, because they feared for their safety?"

"None of us know for sure what other people are thinking—or *were* thinking centuries ago. Perhaps some were driven by imperialistic motives. If they were, they were wrong, and the Koran does not honor their deeds. But you must understand that Christians have done the same thing. Remember that during the Crusades, Christian warriors invaded Muslim lands and shed Muslim blood in order to claim those lands for Christianity."

"Jim," Donald spoke up, "I know it's not my turn, but I feel I must address this issue, or else our Sucher will misunderstand."

"Go ahead, Donald."

"Hamid," Donald continued, "I have noticed that Muslims love to defend their religion's firm commitment to violence and warfare by asserting that it is no different from what Christians did during the Crusades. Quite frankly, I admit that the Christian Crusades and the Muslim conquests have some parallels. But, you see, I can say that the Crusades were evil and should never have happened. You, however, cannot say the same of Muslim warfare. You quoted from the Koran. Let's see, I wrote it down. . . . Here it is. You said, 'Fight . . . "until persecution is no more and religion is for Allah only." ' That is in the Koran, right?"

"Yes. Surah 8:39."

"Historically, leading Muslims have interpreted 'until . . . religion is for Allah only' as calling for war until every nation in the world is a Muslim nation. Because, you see, the ummah is not completely safe until the entire earth is one secure Muslim community."

"Donald, let us not try to fool ourselves," Hamid replied. "Every religion that takes itself seriously aims to see the entire world accept its beliefs. Islam is no—"

"I suppose what you say is true. However, you must realize that the means for accomplishing this in Islam is very different from what Christians believe. Islam believes in spreading its influence through bloodshed. The Koran says so, Muhammad taught so, and leading Muslims ever since have believed so. Many Muslims today do not talk that way because they know that they do not have the military capability to make it happen.

> *Islam believes in spreading its influence through bloodshed. The Koran says so, Muhammad taught so, and leading Muslims ever since have believed so.*
> ~Donald

And they are content to wait until that capability comes about. Some Muslims, however, believe that the Muslim community can be 'made safe' with little military power used strategically and with stealth. And we call them *Muslim terrorists!*"

"Islam does not support terrorism!" Hamid was definitely angry.

"The Koran teaches that Muslims should fight to make the earth one Muslim ummah, and it states that warfare is a good means for accomplishing that goal. You may disagree with the way in which these extremists have chosen to wage their war. But you cannot deny that the Koran permits—no, *demands*—the shedding of blood to make Islam the religion of the *world*."

"Donald, your statements are inaccurate and exceedingly offensive. Jim, I say we end this exchange and move on."

"Hamid, you've got to be kidding," I broke in. "This is the sort of thing I came here for. Donald, let me ask you a question. You said that the Crusades should never have happened. Why?"

"Because the Crusades sought to expand the kingdom of Christ through warfare—as the Muslims have always preferred to do. Christ Himself, however, taught His disciples differently. When Pilate questioned Jesus, concerned that He was going to try to incite violent rebellion, Christ told Pilate, 'My kingdom is not of this world: if my kingdom were of this world, then would my servants fight.'

"At this point we should all understand that the spread of Christianity stands in stark contrast to the spread of Islam. The history of the church from Pentecost to the rise of Emperor Constantine records a series of fierce persecutions. The opposition came as no surprise to Christians, for the Lord had warned them of the world's hatred. But rather than empowering them with weapons for war, Christ gave them His Spirit and His words (consider Matthew 10:19 and Acts 1:8). Despite incredible obstacles and opposition, Christianity multiplied throughout the Roman world until it saturated the empire and persuaded even the emperor himself to be converted.

"Now, let's consider Islam. This religion had its birth in A.D. 610, when Muhammad began receiving his revelations. By the early 700s Islam claimed a solid swath of land from Iran to Spain. But Islam's spread was nothing like Christianity's. Muslims did not spread their beliefs by patiently testifying of their God while being persecuted. They spread their faith through jihad. And this was really the same means that men have used to establish empires since the beginning of history. However, humanly speaking, there was no reason for anyone to become a Christian after the crucifixion of Jesus of Nazareth. The fact that Christian conversion nonetheless conquered the Roman world testifies to the fact that Christianity is no human religion. It is supernatural."

"But, Donald," Hamid protested, "the fact is that Christians *have* defended the Crusades, even if you don't."

"Yes, Hamid, but the testimony of Christ in the New Testament demonstrates that the Crusades were not Christian. At that point in history, Christians failed because they were imitating *Muslims* rather than their Lord. I'd say the Crusades were a Muslim way of dealing with a Christian problem."

"There is nothing Muslim about shedding the blood of those who are steadfast in Allah's way."

"And I would say that you are not able to prove that Muhammad was Allah's prophet. Indeed, the fact that Muhammad could make his religion succeed only by using warfare—while Christianity succeeded without war—seriously damages your ability to convince me of anything that the Christian Scriptures deny."

"Jim," Hamid said, "I believe that it is Shlomo who is supposed to be questioning me. Is that not correct?"

"Indeed. Donald, you've talked long enough. Shlomo?"

"I'm finished," Shlomo replied.

"OK," I said, "let's hear from Javier then."

"Hamid," Javier said, clearing his throat, "you do not believe that Jesus came to die for sin. You don't even believe that Jesus died that day on Golgotha. So my question to you is, If there is no atonement for sin, how can God (or Allah) forgive people of their sin?"

"I see your point, Javier," I interrupted. "What you say about the importance of the atonement is definitely a weak point for both Shlomo and Hamid. I don't think we need to cover that again. Donald, what's your take on Hamid's presentation?"

"Haven't I already interacted with Hamid?" Donald asked.

"Well, I thought you were just helping out Shlomo. I guess you don't have to get involved again."

"Well, I certainly do have more objections."

"Figures!" Jim sort of growled.

"Hamid," Donald began, "it seems to me that there is quite a contradiction between the Koran's positive view of Jesus and its rejection of His claims. I'd like to explore that for a few minutes."

"I can tell you," Hamid was quick to respond, "that Muslims place great value on what Jesus taught and did. He was a great prophet and is considered Allah's Messiah."

"OK," Donald said thoughtfully, "let's talk about Jesus as the Messiah. The word *messiah* means 'anointed one,' in the sense of being designated to accomplish a special task. So, in your understanding of Islam, what special task was Jesus anointed to accomplish?"

"To reveal to mankind things about Allah and his world."

"And where do we learn about what Jesus revealed?"

"The Koran points to the 'Gospel.'"

"The four Gospels?"

The Arabic writing inside the Dome of the Rock proclaims that Jesus is the Messiah, God's messenger, but that God never had a child and there is no Trinity.

"Not exactly. Consider these verses." Hamid searched through his Koran. "Surah 5:65–66: 'If only the People of the Scripture . . . had observed the Torah and the Gospel and that which was revealed unto them from their Lord, they would surely have been nourished from above.' So, you see, the Koran takes a very positive view of the 'Gospel' that Jesus gave to the disciples. However, this 'Gospel' (which I will hereafter refer to by its Arabic name, the *Injil*) differed in several ways from what has become the four Gospels. I say this because not long after the verses I just quoted, one reads the following in Surah 5:75: 'The Messiah, son of Mary, was no other than a messenger.' So Jesus was neither God's Son nor the Redeemer of mankind."

"OK, Hamid," Donald began slowly, "does any of the original Injil survive in our four Gospels?"

"Yes, a great deal."

"Would you say that the leading ideas of the four Gospels are the same as those of the Injil?"

"Yes, I think so."

"Well, Hamid, the fact is that the Gospels are dominated by the teaching that Jesus is divine and that He came to die for the sins of His people. I ask you to consider the following verses: Matthew 8:29; 16:16; Mark 1:1; Luke 1:35; John 1:1; 5:16–23; 9:35–38. Each of these passages affirms the deity of Jesus. Now, concerning the purpose of Jesus' coming to earth, look at the overall emphasis of the four Gospels. Out of the eighty-nine chapters that make up these books, twenty-five chapters record the events surrounding His suffering, death, and Resurrection. That's more than a quarter of the contents of the four Gospels; more than one fourth of these books is devoted to discussing *one week* of His life. To me, that is a very powerful observation demonstrating that Jesus' primary purpose in His earthly life was not to teach or to reveal. It was to be the Savior of mankind."

"Well, Donald, then I guess far more of the Christian Gospels has been corrupted than I used to think," Hamid said with a smug grin.

"Hamid, I think what I've demonstrated is that your concept of the Injil is very different from the four Christian Gospels. Now, my question to you is, Where is this Injil?"

"It has been lost," Hamid said in a very matter-of-fact way.

"Well, that's interesting. We have manuscripts of the four Gospels that go back to the second century A.D. And they all teach emphatically that Jesus is the Son of God and that He came to die for the sins of mankind."

"All that proves, Donald, is that the corruption of the original Injil was complete by the time the second century began."

"That certainly is convenient. But surely you realize that your claim is unlikely. Our earliest manuscripts of the Gospels go back to within a few decades of the apostles' lives. That means that these manuscripts were used by men and women who knew the apostles personally. It is unreasonable to suppose that these people would not have noticed that these manuscripts differed fundamentally from what the apostles taught about Jesus. So, for me to be convinced by your very unlikely explanation, I will need some impressive proof—like a copy of the Injil from the first century. But when I ask you to give me that proof, you cannot give me a copy of the Injil *from any century!*"

"I have the *Koran.* The Koran is the word of Allah. And it states that the Injil of Jesus was true, but it also states that Jesus was *neither* Allah's son *nor* the Savior of the world."

"So what we really have here is a disagreement about authority." Donald was now looking at me, though he was still talking to Hamid. "Since you believe that the Koran is from God, you feel compelled to posit the existence of a 'Gospel of Jesus' that disagrees with the four Gospels—even though there is no evidence for its existence. I, however, believe that the Christian Bible is from God. So when I learn that the Koran rejects many of my Bible's claims, I say that the Koran is wrong. And I find your positing of an unproven Injil very dissatisfying. Have I painted an accurate picture?"

> *At the bottom of it all, yes, the difference [between Christianity and Islam] is one of authority.*
> ~Hamid

"At the bottom of it all, yes, the difference is one of authority."

"I have no other questions. Sucher?"

"Thank you for those clarifications, Donald. Well, Jim, that leaves us with Sean."

"Ah, yes, Sucher," Sean began, "I think I'd like to pick up where Donald left off. Hamid, let's talk about just how accurate the Koran is."

"It is completely accurate."

"Yes, well, my question concerns this thing that people call the doctrine of abrogation. What exactly is that?"

"Ah, yes. Let me acquaint you with some of the pertinent Koranic statements. First of all, I should mention that many point to Surah 22:52." Hamid found the verse and then read, " 'Never sent We a messenger or a Prophet before thee but when he recited the message Satan proposed opposition. . . . But Allah abolisheth that which Satan proposeth. Then Allah establisheth His revelations.'

"Now," Hamid continued, clearing his throat and appearing a bit uncomfortable, "what this verse is saying is that all of Allah's prophets have been opposed by Satan. The Devil attempts to destroy Allah's message by placing in the messengers' minds wrong thoughts. The result is that occasionally they spoke or wrote the wrong thing."

"Muhammad too?" Sean asked.

"He is not excluded," Hamid said.

By this time my jaw was on the floor. "Hamid, you've got to be kidding. This calls into question the whole idea of the Koran as a reliable holy book."

"It most certainly does not. You see, the Koran states that Allah clearly communicates what parts are problematic. Let me read for you Surah 2:106: 'Such of Our revelations as We abrogate or cause to be forgotten, We bring in place one better or the like thereof. Knowest thou not that Allah is Able to do all things?' So here we see that some of the revelations must be abrogated, that is, abolished or corrected in some way. But you must understand that Allah does not leave us wondering what is what. It is the *Koran* that abrogates the Koran. A later verse will correct the problematic verse."

"How can you trust the Koran then?" Sean asked.

"Let me remind you how the verse I just read ends: 'Knowest thou not that Allah is Able to do all things?' Who can tell Allah what to do? If Allah chooses to abrogate one part of the Koran with another, Allah is certainly free to do so. And let me hasten to add that it is not a problem for one verse in the Koran to abrogate another verse, because the abrogated verse is not—indeed never was—the word of Allah. It was all along an interpolation from Satan. So, you see, when speaking of abrogation, I do not at all impugn the integrity of Allah. I impugn only those words of Satan that have been inserted into the Koran."

That's when Jenny spoke up. "But, Hamid, we are not here debating *God's* reliability (or Allah's, as you say). It's the reliability of the *Koran* that's the issue. I too think that God is completely trustworthy, but I also believe that the Koran is not. And just now you have admitted that the Koran is not totally reliable. In effect, what you have said is that the Koran contradicts itself."

"The Almighty does not contradict Himself!" Hamid said.

"Indeed He does not," Jenny agreed. "But the Koran does— you yourself have said so. If the Devil can corrupt the Koran, we are forced to look for a holy book *completely* inspired by God. In other words, we need the Christian Scriptures. You know, it's interesting to me that earlier tonight you told our Sucher that it was dangerous for him to remain a Christian. Now, however, I think he knows what the real danger is."

Jenny looked at me with a smile. I couldn't help it; I was smiling too.

"Jenny," Hamid responded, "I think that your blind allegiance to the Christian Bible has hindered your ability to think clearly. Can we not all agree that a book can have a few contradictions and still be completely reliable?"

That's when Jim broke his silence. "Absolutely. Donald, the Koran's doctrine of abrogation and the Bible's view of its own relative accuracy are really quite similar. Isn't that true?"

"No, that's not true, Jim. Proverbs 30:5–6 states, 'Every word of God is pure. . . . Add thou not unto his words, lest he reprove thee, and thou be found a liar.' And II Timothy 3:16 says, 'All scripture is given by inspiration of God.' If you put those two passages together, you find that the Bible teaches it is absolutely flawless. The Bible's view of itself is that it is infallible. The Koran's view of itself is that it's something less than that."

Just a Brother

5

Thursday came sooner than I expected. I knew I had to go to Homer's, and I consoled myself with the thought that I would enjoy it once I got there. It was raining as I drove, and I secretly hoped something would come up that would cancel the meeting. I was simultaneously looking forward to it and dreading it. The thought of going through another emotional roller coaster wasn't appealing.

The old bell that hung over Jim's door rang as I scrambled into Homer's to escape the rain. Everyone was there. They were all relaxing around the coffee table, seeming not to notice my less-than-graceful entrance. I dropped my bookbag and plopped down on the couch.

"Well, our Sucher has arrived," Jim said, smiling his usual happy smile at me. "We need to begin right away." He turned and looked at Sean expectantly.

Sean said nothing and sat looking reluctant. I remembered hearing something from Jim about Sean's church having reservations about his involvement in our little religious event.

"You've got the spotlight, my friend," Jim said.

Sean took a deep breath and began. "The story of the true Christian faith spans eternity, but I'll try to summarize some of the important aspects. God is a wonderful, loving Heavenly Father who wants us all to be happy and to become just like him. We show our great admiration and worship for our God by desiring to be just like him. This is our glorious privilege, and it is the distinctive of the true Christian church."

69

"Hold on," I interrupted. "Sean, you're a Mormon. Why are you speaking for Christians?"

Sean looked startled at the interruption. "We are the Church of *Jesus Christ* of Latter-day Saints," he answered. "Our faith is in Jesus Christ. People say that Mormons have specific doctrines that are different from the rest of 'Christianity.' But do we all have to agree doctrinally to be considered Christians? According to that logic, Baptists, Presbyterians, and Nazarenes couldn't call each other Christian."

I looked at Sean's earnest face and felt a little sick. He sure seemed sincere about trusting in Jesus. I began to wonder if maybe our beliefs weren't all that different.

But then Jenny piped up. "Don't be ridiculous, Sean. Mormons have fundamental differences with the rest of Christianity." She paused for a moment. "Look, why don't you start your presentation by telling us what your church teaches about God? That should make the point that Christians and Mormons are different. For example, do you believe there is only one God?"

Now Zeezrom said: Is there more than one God?

And he answered: No.

~The Book of Mormon,
Alma 11:28–29

"Yes," Sean replied. "Alma 11:28–29 from our Book of Mormon teaches that there is only one God."

Jenny raised her eyebrows. "Sean," she said, focusing her question, "do you believe that there is no other God who has ever existed or ever will exist?"

Sean stretched his skinny arms above his head and cracked his knuckles loudly before answering. "Well, no, we don't believe that, but neither should you. Don't you believe I Corinthians 8:5?

GET THE BIG PICTURE

Mormon Doctrine

I. The Mormon View of God
II. The Mormon View of Scripture
III. The Mormon View of God's Plan in History
IV. The Mormon View of Christ and Salvation

'There be gods many, and lords many.' The Bible clearly shows there are many gods, and revelation given to later Mormon prophets shows that there are an infinite number of them. Each god is omnipotent, all-knowing, and sovereign. They rule over their own worlds or universes. There's only one God for us, however. We don't have any dealings with the others."

"I noticed you quoted I Corinthians 8:5 without any reference to the context," Jenny said, rolling her eyes. "That's almost a certain sign that you missed the real meaning."

Jim interrupted. "Fachmann Sean, tell us more about the Mormon conception of God."

As man now is, God once was; as God now is, man may be.

~Sean, quoting the Mormon prophet Lorenzo Snow

Sean nodded. "Well, as I said at the beginning, Heavenly Father wants us to become like himself. He truly loves us and thus wants us to have everything he has. That is why we were born, so we could live the way he wants and eventually become as he is. One of our prophets put it this way: 'As man now is, God once was; as God now is, man may be.' "

"What do you mean by that?" I asked. It sounded weird.

"God was once a man like us. He lived in a different world and had his own father. He grew in holiness, righteousness, and sanctification until he progressed to godhood, was glorified, and was given the right to create his own universe, populating it with his own children. We are all his children, and his desire is for us to achieve the same glory he has. We all can achieve godhood as Heavenly Father has."

Sean paused and noticed everyone's negative expressions. He continued defensively. "You shouldn't have any problem with this. Psalm 82:6 says, 'Ye are gods; and all of you are children of the most High.' Your own Bible confirms what I'm saying."

There was a momentary pause. I hadn't expected a Mormon to know verses in my Bible that I was unaware of. Then I remembered Jenny's statement about interpreting in context.

"I don't think you quoted that verse in context either, Sean," I said. "How do I know you're not twisting the meaning of it?"

71

1. God standeth in the congregation of the mighty; he judgeth among the gods.
2. How long will ye judge unjustly, and accept the persons of the wicked? Selah.
3. Defend the poor and fatherless: do justice to the afflicted and needy.
4. Deliver the poor and needy: rid them out of the hand of the wicked.
5. They know not, neither will they understand; they walk on in darkness: all the foundations of the earth are out of course.
6. I have said, **Ye are gods; and all of you are children of the most High.**
7. **But ye shall die like men,** and fall like one of the princes.
8. Arise, O God, judge the earth: for thou shalt inherit all nations.

I noticed Donald nodding his head. He opened his Bible and pushed it across the coffee table to me. I quickly scanned the psalm and immediately noticed that it gave a very different impression from how Sean made it sound. "Sean," I said, "this psalm seems to be sarcastically calling really bad people 'gods.' It says they will die like men and that God will judge them. I don't think it means what you think it means."

Jenny spoke up. "Sean, your doctrine of multiple true gods and eternal progression to godhood is diametrically opposed to the historic teaching of both Judaism and Christianity." I noticed Donald and Shlomo were nodding their heads in agreement.

Mormonism is restored Christianity.

~Sean

"I can't help it if you haven't recognized the truth for two thousand years," Sean said with a shrug. "You're only proving that Mormonism is restored Christianity. It is Christianity in its purest form."

"Wait a second," Jenny replied. "No one taught the eternal progression doctrine until your founder Joseph Smith started teaching it."

Sean looked indignant. "First of all, Jesus Christ founded the church, and Joseph Smith only received the revelation. Second, the prophet was the first to teach the truth because Christ chose to reveal it to him at that time. So who cares if it's new?"

At this point, Jim went to get refreshments. I noticed that Hamid had hardly even moved throughout the discussion. He just sat looking at Sean. I was suddenly glad he wasn't the al-Qaida type. Jim brought us some weird herbal tea that tasted like grass, and Jenny restarted the conversation.

"Sean, your church's teachings depend on what Joseph Smith said."

"No," Sean replied with irritation. "Our teachings depend on the truthfulness of Christ."

"But it was Joseph Smith who told you what Christ supposedly said, correct?" Jenny asked.

"Well, of course."

"How do you know that Joseph Smith was right when he said all these things?" she asked again.

Sean shrugged his shoulders. "The prophet proved that he was a true prophet, seer, and revelator when he translated the plates of Nephi."

Suddenly Jim interrupted. "Let's focus this conversation a little. Sean, why don't you tell us what's so important about these plates." Jim looked at Jenny and me and said, "Right now just let Sean explain some things. If you want to ask a question about what Mormons believe, fine. But we need to save the debating for later."

Sean began. "Well, the plates of Nephi tell us of the continuing plan of God down through the ages. They are another testament of Jesus Christ, much like the New Testament. The plates, now known as the Book of Mormon, help us understand most of what we know about God. Without the Book of Mormon, we would have only the insufficient and corrupted revelation found in the Bible."

"I'm beginning to notice a recurring theme here," I said with a glance at Hamid, who maintained his stony face.

Sean went on. "Well, yes. The Bible is true inasmuch as it was transmitted correctly. And we all know there are many errors in it because of copyists' mistakes and copyists' doctrinal bias. The Book of Mormon actually presents the true teaching of Christ that was lost to the world when the Old and New Testaments were corrupted. Anyway, let me briefly survey the Book of Mormon's story. It tells of Heavenly Father's dealings with an ancient Jewish family that escaped Jerusalem in 600 B.C., only a few years before Jerusalem's destruction by Nebuchadnezzar."

A loud sigh came from Shlomo, who was shaking his head with his eyes shut and a grimace on his face. He was the picture of distaste.

Sean continued. "Lehi and his sons Nephi and Laman and their families left Jerusalem and traveled south, away from Judah. They lived in the desert for long months, dwelling in tents. Then God promised to bring them to the promised land, a land better than all others. Lehi's son Nephi loved his father and his father's God; and God revealed to Nephi many secret truths, which he wrote down on the metal plates. He heard many prophecies concerning the Messiah, many that describe Christ better than any Old Testament prophecy. Nephi's brother Laman, however, resisted God and hated Nephi. Eventually, God commanded Nephi to build a ship, and they all crossed the Atlantic with their father, Lehi, to the promised land, the Americas. Over time their descendants populated North America, or possibly only part of it. They became the Nephites and the Lamanites.

"The two nations, after Nephi's death, were enemies. But the Nephites tried to convert the Lamanites to the true worship of God, even though the Lamanites were hard-hearted and determined to continue in wickedness. God sent prophets to the Nephites to keep them right with him until Christ would come. These prophets took up the task from Nephi of recording the Nephite history on the metal plates. God was doing all this to reveal his truth in its purest form through the Nephite prophets. If you read the Book of Mormon, you'll find its teachings to be much clearer and more precise than the corresponding teachings in the Bible."

"So what happened next?" Jenny asked patiently.

"Well, the plates tell of the kings who reigned over the Nephite people. They took on the responsibility of recording the history of their people. There were good kings and bad kings. God sent prophets to warn the kings and to prophesy about Christ. There were many conflicts between the Lamanites and the Nephites. God continually blessed the Nephites, and prophets arose to keep the Nephites right with him."

"Where's all this going?" I asked. "It seems like a meandering plot."

"You need to be patient, Sucher. You see, God had told Nephi that Jesus Christ would come to his descendants. That's where this is going. Down through the years, God continually reassured the prophets that the Savior would come. But God also predicted that hundreds of years after the Savior came, the Nephites would almost completely apostatize and subsequently be destroyed by the Lamanites."

"That doesn't sound too encouraging. You'd think that Christ's coming would be good news," I said.

"You think that only because you haven't listened to the rest of the story. Christ was planning to do something even better in the latter days. Anyway, after the Resurrection in Palestine, Christ came to the Americas. Both the Nephites and the Lamanites became righteous as they followed Christ's teachings. They loved one another and had everything in common. But about two hundred years after Christ left, both groups deteriorated morally. They soon became completely evil so that only a few were left who followed Christ. The land was overcome with war and bloodshed until all the Nephites were killed, except Mormon and his son Moroni.

"The great prophet Mormon died, and his son Moroni was the last prophet to handle the plates. Here's where we get to see God's great plan for the latter days. Moroni wrote in Mormon 8:14–32 that the record of his

A statue of Moroni stands atop most Mormon temples, such as this one in San Diego, California.

Joseph Smith—first prophet, seer, and revelator of the Church of Jesus Christ of Latter-day Saints

people would come to light in the latter days. Jesus said in III Nephi 16:7 that the fullness of the gospel, that is, the message found in the Book of Mormon, would come to the Gentiles in the last times. And this is exactly what has happened! You see, in 1823 the now-angelic Moroni told the prophet Joseph Smith that he would find the plates of Nephi. It's incredible, but God was planning on restoring the long-lost truth to mankind, just as was prophesied! Joseph Smith found the plates buried in the hill Cumorah in western New York, where Moroni had buried them over a thousand years earlier. The prophet miraculously translated them into English from the reformed Egyptian in which they were written. The result was the Book of Mormon, published in 1830. Finally, man had the fullness of the everlasting gospel restored to him again."

Jenny made a comment. "All that 'history' sounds like an elaborate justification of Joseph Smith's claim to be a prophet."

Sean's face darkened, but he ignored her and continued. "In the Book of Mormon, God often spoke to man through his prophets, so God continued this kind of ministry by giving revelations to Joseph Smith, who was the first in a line of latter-day prophets. God showed Joseph Smith things that hadn't been communicated completely in the Book of Mormon. Much of what the Mormon Church practices today came from these revelations. The revelations about the priesthood, celestial marriage, and eternal progression all came later, though they were contained in germ form in the Book of Mormon. This latter-day prophetic activity is proof that we are the true church.

"God told the prophet that the true church of Jesus Christ was to be re-instituted now that the truth had been restored to man. So Joseph Smith and other men such as Oliver Cowdery and David Whitmer obeyed God and reorganized the true church in 1830 in upstate New York. People soon began to flock to Joseph Smith. Many were from other religious backgrounds; when they read the

Book of Mormon, they recognized in it the truth that they had never found in the Methodist or Baptist churches.

"Unfortunately, the latter-day church, despite its amazing early growth, experienced persecution. Thus, the prophet led them away from New York to Kirtland, Ohio, where they built a temple and stayed for much of the 1830s. Persecution drove the prophet from Ohio to Independence, Missouri. Due to violence, fifteen thousand Mormons were driven from Missouri in 1839 and went to Illinois, where the prophet founded Nauvoo by the Mississippi River. The Mormons established a thriving community and built another temple, but their troubles followed them. People were afraid of the Mormons and wouldn't tolerate their success and what seemed to them to be strange doctrines. Resentment against Mormons grew so great that in 1844 a mob formed when Joseph Smith was in Carthage, Illinois, and the prophet was shot to death, a martyr for Christ.

A mob formed . . . and the prophet was shot to death.

"After Joseph Smith's death, the Mormons followed their new leader, Brigham Young, to what is now Utah, where the Mormon Church is centered today. Young took up the mantle of prophet, seer, and revelator; and he faithfully led the true church of Christ to new levels of greatness. By the time he died in 1877, there were over a hundred thousand Mormons living in Utah, and hundreds of settlements had sprung up, not only in Utah but in neighboring territories as

The temple grounds in Salt Lake City, circa 1896. The temple was dedicated in 1893, just three years before Utah became the forty-fifth state. Utah was established as a territory in 1850 with Young as the first governor.

well. Today, we have millions of members worldwide and temples in America, Korea, Sweden, the Netherlands, Ukraine, Australia, Peru—over a hundred temples all over the world."

Sean stopped talking and looked like he was finished. I started trying to think of a question to ask, but Jenny beat me to it. "Sean, what exactly does your church teach about Jesus Christ? Is He just another one of your millions of gods?"

"Well, yes, in a manner of speaking. He's the firstbegotten of Heavenly Father and was mighty in power and truth in the pre-existence. He was the spirit being chosen to bring salvation to the rest of mankind. He was carried by the virgin Mary, was born, lived a life of goodness and love, and died on the cross to provide the atonement."

"So you believe Christ is equal with the Father?" I asked.

"Yes."

I thought for a moment because I knew there was more to it than this. Then I asked, "Has He always been equal with the Father?"

"Well, no. He was a spirit child just like all of us were. But because he was exceedingly good, he achieved godhood before he was even born in this world. He was a perfect choice to be the one to provide the atonement."

"Wasn't there someone else who wanted to provide the atonement?" Jenny asked with a knowing look.

Sean looked a little uncomfortable, but after a momentary pause he went on. "Yes, Lucifer wanted to provide the atonement, but he was rejected because he wanted to do it in a way that would deny men their free will."

Jenny was nodding her head. "Yes, and who exactly was Lucifer—a spirit child too? One of the Father's children, like Jesus?"

"Yes, but he was against Heavenly Father from the beginning."

"OK," I said. "So Jesus came to earth and died to provide salvation. Some of this sounds like what *I* believe."

"Yes, that's right, Sucher," Jim said, smiling. "There's more agreement than disagreement."

"Um, I don't think so," Jenny said with skepticism. "Let's keep digging here. Sean, what did Christ save people from?"

"Well, all men have sinned. People who sin need to be saved from the consequences, that is, damnation."

"Sounds like Christianity," Jim said with a smile in my direction.

"Well, that's true on the surface," Jenny said. Then she asked, "Sean, what's damnation?"

"Damnation is failing to live in the presence of the Lord. The atonement of Christ paid the penalty for sin so that men can strive for salvation and possibly enter the celestial kingdom of God, where they may shine as the sun in its glory."

"Whoa," I said. I had all kinds of red flags in my mind. "Did you say 'strive for salvation'?"

"That's right. Christ's atonement actually makes a way for us to be able to work out our salvation. Before, we had no hope of salvation; but now, because Christ died for our sins, if we just believe, repent, and are baptized, we can actually have hope of entering the celestial kingdom and enjoying the loving presence of Heavenly Father. Damnation is anything less than enjoying this abundance."

"Damnation is . . . what did you say?" This was me, of course.

"Damnation is anything less than the enjoyment of the celestial kingdom. There are two other kingdoms, of course, the terrestrial and the telestial. These kingdoms are glorious too, but they fall far short of the glory of the celestial. The celestial is like the sun in its glory, the terrestrial is like the moon, and the telestial is like the stars. Those who are moral in this life will go to the terrestrial kingdom and will enjoy the celestial only as from a distance. And they will never be married in eternity. They will enjoy the presence of the Son, but not the Father. Those who are sensual and wicked in this life will enjoy the telestial kingdom (God's mercy is great!). This kingdom is lesser than the other two, but still it is a kingdom of glory. Without the atonement of Christ, no one would be able to enter any of these kingdoms."

"So you consider going to the other two kingdoms to be damnation?" I asked.

"Right. There are varying degrees of damnation. In a sense, the damned in the terrestrial and telestial kingdoms are saved, but it's a partial salvation. They are kind of in the middle."

"Damnation doesn't sound all that bad," I observed out loud. "Sean," I continued, "how does someone get into the really good kingdom?"

"Well, you have to believe in the truth of the fullness of the everlasting gospel and repent and be baptized. Christ's gracious atonement has opened up the way to full remission of sins, as long as we obey the laws and ordinances of the gospel, as our articles of faith put it."

"What are the laws and ordinances?" Jenny asked.

"They are the principles and commandments found in the Book of Mormon and those given by the latter-day prophets. A person must join the Mormon Church to be ultimately saved. One of our apostles, Bruce McConkie, said, 'Those who join the true Church and keep their covenants gain salvation in the celestial kingdom.' "

"I've heard that marriage somehow figures into all this. What is that all about?" I asked.

"Well, to quote our apostle again, 'Baptism is the gate to the celestial kingdom; celestial marriage is the gate to an exaltation in the highest heaven within the celestial world.' Once a person is in the Mormon Church, if he marries another true believer in a temple and they both keep the laws and ordinances of the gospel, they have the hope of eternal godhood themselves, populating their own world with spirit children and ruling as gods."

"What about hell?" I asked. "Do you believe in the lake of fire?"

"Yes, we do. But only the worst offenders, the sons of perdition, will go there forever. They are people who are in league with the Devil. Most people will end up in the telestial kingdom."

"Sean," Jenny said, "you said that repentance and baptism are required for salvation in the celestial kingdom. What exactly are repentance and baptism?"

Mormonism's View of Personal Eschatology (The Fate of Individuals)

Kingdoms of Glory

Celestial Kingdom

Highest Heaven

In addition to fulfilling the requirements for entrance into the lower levels of celestial glory, those who partake of celestial marriage will enjoy godhood in the highest heaven of the celestial kingdom, populating their own worlds with spirit children.

Lower Levels of Glory

For those who . . .

- Repent
- Are baptized by the proper Mormon official
- Obey Mormon teaching
- Experience justification after a righteous life

Terrestrial Kingdom

For those who live morally but not according to Mormon teaching

Telestial Kingdom

For those who live sensually and wickedly

The Lake of Fire (Hell, and/or Outer Darkness)

The sons of perdition (Satan and his angels, apostates from Mormonism, and extremely wicked people)

Damnation

"Repentance is turning from your sins, making restitution for any wrongs you have committed, and changing your ways. Baptism is the ordinance in which a person is immersed in water by the proper official of the Mormon Church."

"So salvation is found in the Mormon Church," I said.

"Yes, it is the true church of Jesus Christ upon the earth. As prophesied in the Book of Mormon, God's latter-day activity is found in the church. All other churches don't contain the purity of the true faith. The greatest degree of salvation people in other churches can hope for is in the terrestrial kingdom."

"That's the one where we're unmarried moons, right?" I asked.

Sean laughed. "No, your glory in that kingdom is like the moon reflecting the sun. And you will remain unmarried in that kingdom." He got serious again. "I know that as I've been talking, you must have sensed the compelling nature of the prophets' revelations. Join yourself to the one true church on earth so that you can enjoy celestial bliss forever."

"So, if I join the Mormon Church, get baptized, find a great Mormon babe, and tithe regularly, I'll be set for godhood?" I was at the height of my skepticism.

Sean looked mildly annoyed, but before he could reply, Jenny abruptly changed the subject. "Can we get a little more specific about your doctrine of salvation? What do you believe about justification? Oh, wait; I probably need to define the term for Steve."

Sometimes Jenny thinks a bit much of herself. "I don't need it defined," I retorted. "I know it means when God makes a person righteous."

Sean smiled, "Well, Steve, you're close. The atonement of Christ makes it possible for men to become more and more righteous through life by obeying the laws and ordinances of the gospel. If a person persists in obedience, the Holy Spirit declares him righteous based on his life of righteousness. Justification is God's pronouncement of his righteousness after he's lived a life that is righteous. It's not that God made him righteous, but God made a way for him to live a righteous life and to be declared to be what he really is at the end. God is not going to declare somebody to be something that he isn't. He isn't going to give someone a righteous standing who hasn't earned it."

This answer confused me. I looked at Jenny and then at Donald. But before we could continue, Jim spoke up. "I think we're about out of time on this one. Let's take a break before roasting Fachmann Sean." We all agreed.

Can We Become Gods?

6

Memory Verse: Isaiah 44:8

After our break, I decided to ask Hamid to start first. I was interested to find out what a Muslim thought about Mormonism.

He began to speak slowly, his accent thick. "Sean, is your God the ultimate power in the universe?"

Sean looked like he thought the answer was obvious. "Yes, of course. God is omnipotent and the greatest being there is."

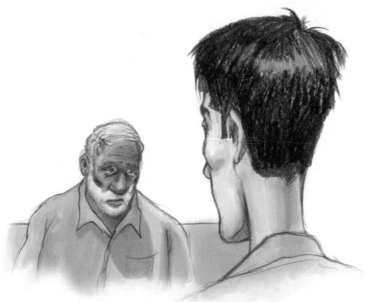

Hamid shook his head. "Your concept of God fails to meet this necessary attribute that the one true God must fulfill."

"Oh really?" Sean replied with skepticism.

Hamid went on to explain. "God must be ultimate. Your concept of an eternal progression to godhood miserably fails to provide for an ultimate God. According to you there is an infinite

GET THE BIG PICTURE

Examining Mormon Doctrine

I. Examining the Mormon View of God
II. Examining the Mormon View of Scripture
III. Examining the Mormon View of Christ and Salvation

regress of gods back into eternity. Each god is contingent upon the previous gods, and thus each god needs the previous gods. But an infinite, omnipotent God cannot *need* anything. He must be self-sufficient. By definition, your gods cannot be ultimate.

"In addition, your universe has a serious moral problem. Your universe is populated (or will be populated) with gods that have sinned. Yes, according to you, they have been glorified to godhood, but what good is a God who has sinned, who has been glorified by another God who sinned, *ad infinitum?* What guarantees that your God will not revert and sin again? He cannot guarantee it because he is not ultimate. And the gods before him can't guarantee it because they are no better than he. Only an ultimate, omnipotent God, who can subject all things to His will, can guarantee anything. Thus, you do not have a perfect, pure, and spotless God for all eternity. A God whose very nature is untemptable. A God who cannot sin and never has. A God who is the ultimate moral standard for the universe.

"In addition to this, who is the determiner for morals in your universe? Your God? No, indeed it cannot be. He has been glorified to a position that is not inherently sinless; he is contingent upon other beings that are like him. They presumably have all either made up their own moral codes for their universes or have submitted to a moral code above themselves. If they submit to a code, then there is an ultimate determiner for morals beyond them, something that is more 'ultimate,' yea, more 'God' than any of them. If they have determined their own morality, then there may be universes or worlds in existence in which evil is considered good. There would be nothing keeping that God from destroying your God. You would have no security. If you answer that your God is omnipotent, so what? The other is also. It would be a clash of the titans, and your God would be busy defending himself from a power as powerful as himself. When two powers meet like this, inevitably those who look on, who are dependent upon one of the powers, get hurt. Where is your security? There is a fundamental weakness in your God. If you answer that nothing like this has ever happened, I say who's to say it isn't about to? If you say there is an agreement between the gods to not allow such a scenario, then I say if the gods determine their own morality, why should the

power-hungry gods keep the agreement? If you say they must, then they are bound by a power greater than themselves.

"Thus, you have no ultimate standard for right and wrong, truth and nontruth. In your scheme of things, there must be an ultimate to govern your so-called ultimate gods. Your gods need a God. This foundational philosophical problem in your worldview shows that it is a failing worldview."

Hamid stopped for a moment and looked down. He had been slowly and methodically reasoning while glancing back and forth between Sean, Jenny, and me. But now he was silent, as though he was trying to decide if he should continue. He decided.

"Let me make one more point. You have a God who is not changeless. He was once a baby, then a man—and a sinner, mind you—and now has achieved omniscience. He has changed. And because you have no access to the ultimate, you have no basis for saying he will not change again. If your God says he won't, then you need to ask how he knows that, and he will have no one to which to appeal in answer. He will have to say, 'Take my word for it.' But because your God is not ultimate, he has no authority to say that. He is a contingent being, and contingent beings cannot say things for sure, because they need someone who transcends

A single ultimate God rules.

them to determine what is true and not true. As a matter of fact, your God seems to delight in changing. Your church has been known to say that some things are everlasting decrees but then later get revelation from your God that he's changed his mind. This is, I suppose, consistent with your worldview, but it's a very poor God that you serve. In Islam, Allah cannot change; his origins are from everlasting, and he has never changed in his decisions about what is right and wrong, what is true and what is not true. He is the ultimate who is the uncaused cause, who cannot change, who is not contingent upon anything or anyone, who cannot be defeated or overruled, and who has all authority to dictate morals and truth to man."

"Wow, fascinating," I said. *I need to hear it again for it to make sense,* I thought.

Everyone else (except for Sean, who looked confused) seemed to have understood what Hamid had said. I quickly asked Shlomo to speak next.

Shlomo began. "I totally agree with Hamid. At least there's one thing a Jew and a Muslim can agree upon. Your claim that Mormonism is a monotheistic religion redefines the meaning of monotheism. Mormonism is nothing more than polytheism."

Sean looked uncomfortable, but he managed to respond. "Well, there are other gods, but there is only one God with whom *we* have to do. So for us, God is ultimate enough, and the other gods don't really matter."

"I don't see how you can say that in light of what Hamid just said." Shlomo went on. "You have no certain, ultimate source for truth. You can say that your prophet's word is sufficient because he speaks for God, but your God's words aren't sufficient because he is only an 'omnipotent' being in the company of an infinite number of 'omnipotent' beings. It's ludicrous even to speak of multiple omnipotent beings. Multiple beings can't each have all power. If one has all the power, then there's nothing left for the others to have."

Shlomo continued. "I don't want to just reiterate Hamid's points. Sean, what is your opinion of the book of Isaiah?"

"It's one of the greatest prophecies in the Old Testament," Sean replied. "Multiple chapters are quoted by Book of Mormon authors because of its beauty and depth."

"Indeed, but Mormons need to pay more attention to the parts of Isaiah that the Book of Mormon fails to mention."

At this, Shlomo reached into his coat and retrieved a medium-sized black volume from some deep pocket. "This is a Hebrew Tanakh. Feel free to follow along in your English version. I'll translate as I read Isaiah 44:6."

Sean appeared not to have noticed Shlomo's invitation. Donald opened his Bible and waited expectantly. Javier, though he had a Bible, did not open his; he just sat looking suspicious. Hamid didn't have a Bible, just a Koran. His eyes were focused and interested. Jenny opened a Bible she pulled off the shelf, but Jim seemed to lose interest.

> *This is what the Lord says, the King of Israel and Israel's redeemer, the Lord of armies. I am the first and I am the last. There is no God except for me.*
> ~Shlomo, translating Isaiah 44:6

"Take a look at this verse. It says, 'This is what the Lord says, the King of Israel and Israel's redeemer, the Lord of armies. I am the first and I am the last. There is no God except for me.' Now look at verse 8. 'Is there a God except for me? Indeed, there is no God. I know of none.'"

"The Bible is correct only if it's transmitted properly," responded Sean. "Either that's a corrupt text or you're misunderstanding it."

Shlomo was ready for this. "Sean, no one denies that the hundreds of manuscripts of the Tanakh have minor variants in them.

But this is a far cry from the Mormon teaching that the Tanakh was corrupted and no longer contains much of the original teaching. This is simply misinformation. There is absolutely no textual evidence for it."

"Who needs evidence? We have the prophet's word."

"Well, Sean," Shlomo said patiently, "your worldview contains foundational philosophical problems. And your source of truth makes blanket statements about known historical reality that are completely unable to be substantiated; you just accept your prophet's word without historical evidence. However, God's descriptions of history in the Tanakh fit historical reality because they are historically real, and thus man can find evidence for them in archeology and ancient literature. Joseph Smith's comments about the Tanakh being corrupt do not agree with historical reality at all—let me emphasize— AT ALL. Look at the manuscript evidence and its preservation, and you will realize that we have the Law, the Prophets, and the Writings just as they were given."

Torah Scroll
From the Bob Jones Museum & Gallery Bowen Collection of Antiquities

Sean looked like he was calming himself. "Well, Mormons have the Holy Ghost to aid our understanding. We're not stuck with revelation given thousands of years ago."

"OK then," Shlomo said, "why don't you tell us your 'divinely aided' understanding of Isaiah 44:6 and 8?"

Sean ignored the blast of sarcasm and thought for a moment. "It simply means that God knows of no other God in this world. He's not saying there are no other gods at all."

"It says, 'There is no God except for me.' How can you miss the plain meaning of that, Sean?"

"I have further revelation clarifying such ambiguous texts."

Shlomo shook his head and leaned back into his seat. His look at Jim and me communicated that he was finished. I looked at Javier and Donald. Javier didn't look as eager to engage in the discussion as Donald, so I asked Donald to go next.

"Sean, do you consider your scriptures to be truth? Do you consider what your scriptures say to be absolute and unchanging?"

"Yes, of course," Sean replied. "They were given by God."

Donald nodded. "Sean, as Hamid said, the Mormon God is not ultimate. The Mormon scriptures supposedly come from this God who is not ultimate. Thus, your scriptures are not necessarily ultimate truth. Your God and thus your revelation lack a central stabilizing base."

"Our scriptures can't be wrong because they were given by an all-knowing God who can't lie," Sean retorted.

Donald was quick to respond. "I don't think you have a basis for asserting anything about this God, because you have no certain source of information. Your God is not ultimate; therefore, he cannot assert absolute truth."

Donald looked at Jim. "Now I'd like to discuss the Mormon view of revelation. Do you have the two sets of Mormon writings called *History of the Church* and the *Journal of Discourses*?"

Jim looked surprised but muttered that he did. "I can't get anyone to buy them." He scurried off and presently brought Donald an old cardboard box full of dog-eared and weather-stained hardback books. They were organized neatly. Definitely Jenny's influence. Jim immediately made chaos out of them by taking them out and setting them haphazardly on the coffee table. As Jim unpacked the many volumes, Donald went on.

"I studied Mormonism years ago for a comparative religions class I taught on the college level. I read through the Book of Mormon and some other Mormon documents. Oh, and Jim, could you please get me a Book of Mormon, *Doctrine and Covenants, Pearl of Great Price,* and McConkie's *Mormon Doctrine*?"

"Sure," Jim replied.

Jim presently returned with more books, which he tossed onto the coffee table.

Now armed to the teeth with books, Donald looked at the rest of us. "Before I show you a few items from this literature, I want to state what I'm driving at. When a prophet suddenly appears after eighteen hundred years and adds all this revelation to the Bible—revelation that radically changes foundational doctrine, revelation that does not fit in with the plan of history presented in the Bible but actually presents a completely different plan—then Bible believers have the right to seriously question that prophet. We are actually commanded to do so in Deuteronomy 18:20–22.

"Although there are many issues, I will discuss three: Joseph Smith's credibility, discrepancies among the Mormon prophets, and problems in the Book of Mormon itself.

"Joseph Smith has a major credibility problem." Donald picked through the pile of books on the table. "Ah, here it is. This is Smith's *History of the Church,* in which Smith chronicles the 'continuing work of God in the earth.' This is volume 6. Let's see here; I think the quote is pretty far into the book."

We all waited a few moments until Donald found what he was looking for. Almost everyone looked interested except Sean, who looked tense and apprehensive.

"OK, I've found the quote on pages 408–409. Remember, the point I'm making concerns Smith's credibility. Sean, you said that your faith is in Jesus Christ; but after further questioning, you admitted that you trust Joseph Smith's testimony as to what Jesus said. You trust that Smith was simply a humble servant of his master, Jesus Christ. Well, listen to this statement from Smith himself.

> I have more to boast of than ever any man had. I am the only man that has ever been able to keep a whole church together since the days of Adam. A large majority of the whole have stood by me. Neither Paul, John, Peter, nor Jesus ever did it. I boast that no man ever did such a work as I. The followers of Jesus ran away from Him; but the Latter-day Saints never ran away from me yet."

Donald paused a moment after he finished reading. "I think this statement needs no comment; it speaks for itself." He put the book down and looked around at all of us.

Brigham Young

"Although there is much more that could be said about Smith's lack of credibility, let me move on to contradictions among the Mormon prophets. The second prophet, seer, and revelator of the Mormon Church was Brigham Young. He scandalized the Mormon Church with the Adam-God doctrine."

Donald again started looking through his pile of books. He found an old black volume and started thumbing through it. "Here's a doozie. This is the *Journal of Discourses* volume 1, page 50. He's got so many capitalized and italicized words in this paragraph I'd have to yell to get his emphasis across. Don't worry, I won't.

> Now hear it O inhabitants of the earth, Jew and Gentile, Saint and sinner! When our father Adam came into the garden of Eden, he came into it with a *celestial body,* and he brought Eve, *one of his wives,* with him. He helped to make and organize this world. He is MICHAEL, *the Archangel,* the ANCIENT OF DAYS! About whom holy men have written and spoken—He *is our* FATHER *and our* GOD, *and the only God with whom* WE *have to do.*

"Young wrote and preached a lot about Adam being God, but the Mormon Church of today has repudiated this doctrine."

Sean looked upset. "President Young was only theorizing."

Donald smiled. "Well, other statements of his seem to rule out that interpretation. Listen to the statement on the next page.

> Now, let all who may hear these doctrines pause before
> they make light of them, or treat them with indifference,
> for they will prove their salvation or damnation.

"And there's one more in the *Journal of Discourses* volume 13, page 95." He again picked up one of the books and started thumbing through it. "Here it is.

> I have never yet preached a sermon and sent it out to the
> children of men, that they may not call Scripture. Let me
> have the privilege of correcting a sermon, and it is as
> good Scripture as they deserve.

"Now these statements are very difficult for Mormons to deal with. How can they claim a man to be their prophet who they say taught false doctrine? Just as their doctrine of God destabilizes them, this issue gives them no assurance that they can trust those men who demand their confidence.

"OK, let me finish with problems in the Book of Mormon itself. To an untaught ear, it sounds very much like the Bible. It has an archaic sound to it because Smith tried to copy the Elizabethan English of the King James Version of the Bible, despite the fact that he didn't speak that way himself. No one did in the early 1800s. Elizabethan English was the manner of speech in the late 1500s and early 1600s. As a matter of fact, because Smith was not familiar with the language, you can actually find places where he goofed and used 'you' when he should have used 'ye,' for example.

"My main point, however, is that the Book of Mormon does not speak with the same voice as the Bible. Jesus said, 'My sheep hear my voice, and I know them, and they follow me.' My contention is that the Book of Mormon tries to mimic God's voice but is actually the voice of a man."

"Donald," I said, thoroughly confused, "what do you mean by 'voice'? You can't hear anyone when you read it."

"I mean that the Word of God has certain qualities that mark it as what it is—God's Word. Anyone can write something that says, 'Thus saith the Lord.' Nearly every holy book in existence makes such a claim. The fact that the book recounts miracles, discusses great plans of God, tells of fantastic angelic visitations, and contains prophetic utterances doesn't mean that it is from God. These elements are not God's mark."

"Well then, what is?" I asked.

"In Isaiah 41 and 42 God contends that false gods are worthless. God says in Chapter 42 verses 8 and 9,

> I am the Lord: that is my name: and my glory will I not give to another, neither my praise to graven images. Behold, the former things are come to pass, and new things do I declare: before they spring forth I tell you of them.

"Thus, based on these passages, one aspect of God's mark is accurate, fulfilled prophecy."

Sean burst out confidently, "Then the Book of Mormon is of God! It said it would come to light in the last days, and it did."

"Sean, your book has every sign that it is a nineteenth-century document. It would be easy to write it in the nineteenth century and concoct 'prophecies' such as the one you just mentioned to try to put a stamp of authority on it. Convincing prophecies, ones the Lord refers to in Isaiah 42, are those that the author could not have known about in advance without divine help. The Bible has many cases of such fulfilled prophecies, such as Daniel 9:26 and Isaiah 53. And there is no question that these prophecies often predated their fulfillments by hundreds of years."

Donald continued. "As I read the Book of Mormon, I kept an eye out for differences between it and the Bible. You see, the Bible contains marks of the various men who contributed to it— each author's particular style and his own vocabulary. But the Bible has one primary author—God—and therefore it also bears His marks that are typical either of the whole Bible or of whole genres in the Bible. The things I discovered show the differences between the two books and that the Book of Mormon doesn't have the same author as the Bible.

"First, there's the issue of selectivity of material. In the Bible, everything has a purpose. God wastes no words. Every word and every element of the story matters to the theme of the whole. God cares so much about this that all the narratives (in both the Old and the New Testaments) are surprisingly brief to everyone who reads them. There are no superfluous elements added for the personal pleasure of the readers as found in modern stories. God is concise. He cares primarily for the conveyance of meaning, not for excessive detail. This really is not evident in the Book of Mormon. Have you ever watched a drama and thought that if half of the story was cut out of it, the story would be the same? Well, that is evidence of a writer who likes to hear himself talk. He's verbose. This is definitely a characteristic of the Book of Mormon.

"Second, there's the issue of progressive revelation connected by predictive prophecy. The Bible is a linear, united thread. From

beginning to end there is a unity to the story as revelation is progressively given. Each successive part sheds light on previous parts and is necessary for those previous parts to have meaning. The Book of Mormon does not fulfill any previous part of the Bible. It is not part of the wonderful unity that is God's revelation. It's an offshoot that purports to intersect God's salvation history. But God hasn't shown us that He works with offshoots. God has indicated that He works

Joseph Smith, a man with a strong religious imagination with a linear unity.

"Next, there is excessive and indiscriminate use of Old and New Testament language. The author of the Book of Mormon constantly uses phraseology from the various biblical writers. For example, you find Pauline style and phraseology on others' lips. You find illustrations that are peculiar to Paul used often throughout, illustrations such as the olive tree from Romans 11. The Bible never does this. Whenever God quotes Himself, it is for a purpose. He does not repetitively lace subsequent revelation with familiar phrases until those phrases become trite clichés. The impression is that the author of the Book of Mormon tried to borrow the authority of the Bible, weaving it into his fabrication in order to give his writing credibility.

"Last, there's the very significant problem of the Book of Mormon's admitting to the possibility of error. It denies inspiration for itself in I Nephi 19:6, Mormon 8:12, and Mormon 9:33. But according to II Timothy 3:15–16, God's words are inspired."

Then I remembered something Sean had said earlier. "Donald, can you explain Christ's death and justification to us? Was Sean right when he explained it?"

"Thanks for reminding me, Steve. Let's start with justification; the atonement will naturally come up. Steve, you said that justification is God's making someone righteous. And Sean, you said that justification is God's declaration of a man's righteousness after that man has proved that he is."

Sean didn't say anything. He just sat looking like he was ready to have the examination finished.

Donald went on. "Well, Sucher, justification is not God's *making* someone righteous; Sean was right about that. But his teaching that it is God's declaring you righteous after all your effort at making yourself so couldn't be more wrong."

After a glance in Sean's direction, Donald continued. "Anyway, unlike Mormon scriptures, the Bible does have a lengthy treatment of the doctrine of justification—especially in Romans 1–4. Here you have God giving over a hundred verses to the subject. Obviously God is concerned that we understand it. Let's find out what He says. I'll summarize the argument of the first four chapters." Jenny, Javier, Sean, and I had Bibles open as Donald opened his.

"Chapter 1 verses 16–17 give the theme of the book. Starting at verse 18, God begins to explain how it is that righteous people will live by faith. He needed to explain this because the Jews of Paul's day thought that God considered them righteous on the basis of their having the law and obeying it, specifically submitting to the ritual of circumcision.

"Verses 18–32 explain that non-Jews cannot have a righteous standing before God because they suppress the truth and degenerate into wickedness. God's wrath is already revealed against them for this reason. Chapters 2:1–3:8 basically put the Jew under the same condemnation. See especially chapter 2:23–29.

"Then, in chapter 3:9–20, Paul summarizes God's indictment of both Jews and non-Jews. Paul claims that no one is righteous; sin has affected their understanding, their posture towards God, their profit for God, their behavior, their throat, their tongues, their lips, their mouth, their feet, and their ways. All this means that they are totally depraved. Every aspect of their nature has been corrupted so that they are like spoiled milk and good only to be thrown away. This leaves man hopeless of ever being able to be right with God. This is the bad news.

"Verses 21–26 begin the good news by saying that a righteousness of God that is apart from law is available to man. That's in verses 21–22. This righteousness is available to everyone because everyone is condemned and unable to be justified any other way. Do you see that in 22–23? Justification is free and by grace and is found in Christ's redemption. See that in 24? Christ's redemption is described as a propitiation in verse 25, which is a sacrifice given to calm wrath. This tells you that Jesus died on the cross to appease the wrath of God that Romans chapters 1–3 have been describing. God was justly angry with sinners, and Christ died to calm that anger by taking men's sins upon Himself, as I Peter 2:24 says. Verse 25 also says that man gains the benefits of Christ's propitiation by faith, that is, by believing.

"Now, all this is very significant. It refutes Mormonism's idea of what Christ's atonement did for man. The atonement didn't make man able to work his way to a righteous standing. Christ's atonement appeased God's wrath so that if a man simply believes in Christ, he will receive a righteous standing. This is confirmed in verse 28, which says that man is justified by faith without deeds of law. It also debunks the Mormon idea that justification takes place after we make ourselves righteous. Romans 5:1 says explicitly that justification is a past event in the life of a believer in Christ.

"I conclude that the Mormon doctrine of salvation is unscriptural. Justification is God's declaring someone righteous on the basis of the propitiation of Christ and at the point of that person's genuine faith in Christ and in His substitutionary atonement. It is obvious that either Joseph Smith was ignorant of the Bible's teaching on justification or else he deliberately ignored it."

Sean spoke up at this point. "God's oracles are not found in Donald here. I listen to the true church. It is the only source for truth. It is the only church that maintains a prophet, seer, and revelator, and that is the mark of the true church on earth."

The Salt Lake City temple today

Now that Donald was finished, I looked over at Javier. He looked eager, so I nodded to him.

Javier sat up in his seat and looked at Sean. "Do you put more stock in your past scriptures or your present prophet's declarations?" he asked.

Sean looked surprised by this question. He blinked several times and answered, "They are both equally authoritative. I accept both as God's revelation to man."

Javier nodded in understanding. "You know, Sean, I see what you just said as another problem with Mormonism. I've had this in mind during the whole discussion, but I haven't been able to crystallize it until now. Your authority is not really in your scriptures. The present prophet has the right to overrule past scripture." Javier had been flipping through one of the books on the coffee table. He held it up and continued. "For example, I just came across the Mormon apostle Bruce McConkie's treatment of African Americans in his book *Mormon Doctrine*. McConkie tried to organize the Mormon teaching on African Americans in the '50s, but only years later in the '70s, the church suddenly got a 'revelation' that overruled over a hundred years of doctrine on that issue. McConkie's summary of Mormon doctrine on the issue was suddenly obsolete. This fact leaves Mormons with no sense of security in knowing the character of God through a fixed, objective revelation. They are left asking, 'How is the prophet going to change our religion next?' Their authority is in changeable man. I think we must conclude that Mormonism fails the Deuteronomy 18 test that Donald mentioned. Scripture warns that heresies would come. We must assert that Mormonism is one of them."

Just a Creature

7

As I drove to Homer's for another night of our lovely Auseinanderzetsung, I wondered what I would hear from the Jehovah's Witness, Javier. All through the day at school I had burst out in spontaneous expressions of amazement at the Mormon stuff I'd heard from Sean. I kept noticing the Mormon kids I knew and wondered if they were going around anticipating godhood. All the stuff I'd learned about Mormons was difficult to keep to myself, but I did. It didn't seem to be the kind of thing to turn into a joke.

When I arrived at Homer's and made myself comfortable in the old couch, I looked at Javier and realized I was about to see him "get going." Besides hearsay, I didn't know much about Jehovah's Witnesses. I'd always noticed that one of their Kingdom Halls was next door to Fatty's Hamburgers, where I ate sometimes after school. I also had a pushy Witness come to my door once who tried to convince me that God doesn't send people to hell forever. That was pretty much the extent of my experience with them.

"Well, Sucher, are you ready to hear about the Jehovah's Witnesses?" Jim asked, smiling his usual friendly smile.

"Um, sure," I said. "Go ahead, Javier. Why don't you tell us about the history of your religion and then tell us what you believe."

History and Beliefs of the Jehovah's Witnesses

GET THE BIG PICTURE

I. **History**
   A. Reason for Existence
   B. Origins of the Movement

II. **Beliefs**
   A. The Trinity and Christ's Deity
   B. Christ's Atonement and Man's Salvation
   C. End Times and the Individual's Fate

Javier smiled broadly and cleared his throat. "Well, the history of Jehovah's organization corresponds with our teachings, so it will be hard to distinguish them, but I'll try. The issue we must address first is the main purpose of Scripture. The book of Ezekiel says over sixty times that people will know that God's name is Jehovah. From this we gather that God is very interested in His being accurately known in the earth. He is especially interested that people know that His name is Jehovah. He emphasizes in Exodus 3:15 that His name is Jehovah forever 'unto all generations.' This is one of the great sins of Christendom, that they have obscured the divine name. You can actually see how they do it even in their Bible translations."

Javier reached for his copy of the Bible and motioned me to open mine.

"Take a look, for example, at the very well-known passage of Psalm 23. What does the first line say, Steve?"

I was surprised at being questioned, but I went ahead and answered. "It says, 'The Lord is my shepherd.' "

"Yes, that is what your translation says. But what do you notice about the letters in your word *Lord?*"

"That they're in the right order? I don't know. What are you driving at?" I'm sure my tone betrayed that I thought it was a weird question.

Unperturbed, Javier continued. "Just notice that the letters are all capitalized. Now turn to Psalm 110:1. What do you notice about the two occurrences of the word *Lord* here?"

"One *Lord* is in all caps and the other uses lowercase letters," I answered. "I've never noticed that before. What does it mean?"

"I'll tell you what it means, Steve," Javier said, scooting forward to the edge of his seat. "The translators of your version and just about every other major version are obscuring the name of Jehovah. Do you realize that whenever you find the word *Lord* in all caps in your Bible, it is really the divine name of Jehovah in the Hebrew text?"

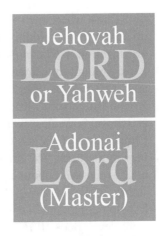

I looked at Donald with a quizzical look, but he simply nodded in assent to what Javier said.

"Don't look to Donald for help on this one, Steve. He knows what I'm saying is true. The churches of Christendom don't want to acknowledge God's true name, so they have obscured it by translating it with another word. It's outright deception."

"Hold it, Javier," Jenny said. "I don't think you can say it is deception. I mean, they did capitalize the word so you could distinguish it from the other word for Lord."

"Oh yes, that is very helpful," Javier said sarcastically. "The problem is that no one ever notices it. Our Sucher here had never noticed it until I just pointed it out to him. Anyway, my point is that the churches of Christendom have hindered and are hindering God's purpose in declaring His name."

Javier took a moment to regain his composure and went on. "God is so intent upon spreading the knowledge of His name in the earth that the coming paradise on earth is described as a time when the knowledge of Jehovah will cover the earth as waters cover the sea; that's Isaiah 11:9. But until then, Jehovah has chosen Witnesses who testify to the truth. The nation of Israel was supposed to carry out this role, as Isaiah 43:10 states. Jehovah God also called various individuals to this role, one being Ezekiel the prophet and another being the Lord Jesus Christ. Jesus Himself said in Revelation 3:14 that He is 'the faithful and true witness.' God has always maintained Witnesses in the earth, those who testify to God's name and make known God's truth.

"That's where the modern-day Witnesses come in. God raised up a man in the middle 1800s, Charles Russell, to begin the new organization. He began what became known as the International Bible Student movement and founded the Watch Tower Bible and Tract Society. Russell died in 1916. In the 1930s, under Joseph Rutherford's leadership, the movement became known as Jehovah's Witnesses in order to distinguish itself from apostate Christendom. This was God's organization on earth to bear witness to the truth. The organization grew steadily and taught the nations the truth about Jehovah, using home Bible studies and a strong publishing arm. The organization published many books to help people understand the Scriptures. Also, two magazines were developed—*Watchtower* (which had existed back in Charles Russell's day) and later *Awake!*—that exist to this day, helping Jehovah's Witnesses learn and apply God's truth to their lives. They are distributed widely by faithful Witnesses as they preach the gospel of the kingdom on doorsteps all over the world.

"One would naturally expect Jehovah to raise up this organization at this time of world distress and religious unfaithfulness. As Ezekiel of old, we have been set as a watchman to the nations, and especially to apostate Christendom. We are to declare the truth and warn those who are heading for destruction by their involvement with the heretical churches of Christendom."

The Jehovah's Witnesses organization views itself as a watchman, warning the world of God's coming judgment.

"OK, hold on, Javier," I said when he took a breath. "How do you know your 'organization' is of God? It sounds like you just assume that you are God's chosen group."

Javier didn't miss a beat. "Well, let me ask you, Steve. Who was it who opened your understanding about Exodus 3:15—that God's name is Jehovah 'unto all generations'? Who is declaring this truth? Do you hear it at your church? No. Do you hear it when you listen to radio preachers? No. You don't hear it anywhere because Christendom is obscuring God's name. And who was it who gave you light concerning the fact that over five thousand times the Old Testament uses the name Jehovah, and yet modern translators obscure it by translating it *Lord,* even though God has said that Jehovah is His name forever? Did the churches of Christendom point this out to you? No, you needed one of Jehovah's true Witnesses to show you God's truth on these vital issues. Thus I believe that if the churches are obscuring these vital truths, and members of the Jehovah's Witnesses are making them known, then it is obvious who God's true organization really is."

I thought a moment after this. Javier did sound knowledgeable, but something about what he was saying sounded hollow. I just couldn't put my finger on it.

Jenny piped up. "Javier, what happened between A.D. 100 and the 1800s? Was everyone in the dark until the Jehovah's Witnesses showed up in the late 1800s? Seems pretty egotistical."

"Well, there were some true Witnesses before. The present-day organization is sort of like a modern-day revival of true Christianity."

"OK," Jim said from behind the counter, "we need to move along. Let's hear what you believe on certain theological issues, Fachmann Javier."

"Yes," Jenny said. "I know you don't believe in the Trinity. Could you tell us why?"

"It will be my pleasure to blow that confusing and unreasonable doctrine out of the water," Javier replied, smiling. "My discussion of the doctrine of the Trinity will again show how Christendom dishonors God and how the Jehovah's Witnesses are God's true organization.

"Let me ask you, would anybody ever get the doctrine of the Trinity from just reading his Bible? No, he wouldn't. It's not taught anywhere in the Bible. The word itself isn't in the Bible. It is a doctrine that was contrived at numerous church councils during the fourth and fifth centuries after Christ.

"As a matter of fact, the Bible itself clearly teaches that the Trinity is a false doctrine. I can prove this best by discussing the issue of the deity of Christ. That's really where the doctrine of the Trinity stands or falls. Take a look at John 17:3. It portrays Jesus praying to God and saying that the Father is 'the only true God.' Now this verse ought to be enough to show that the doctrine of the Trinity is false. If God is the only true God, then no one else can be the only true God. Do you see that, Steve? Do you see how this verse decimates the Trinity doctrine?"

> *And this is life eternal, that they might know thee the only true God, and Jesus Christ, whom thou hast sent.*
> ~John 17:3

I sat motionless. "Well, I need to study it out," I said. "Why don't you go on." I had to admit that what Javier had said spooked me a little. I'd never looked at John 17:3 in that light before. What Javier said seemed to make sense. *If the Father is the only true God, as Jesus said, then how can we say that Jesus is the true God?* I felt confused, but I decided to wait before I tried to figure it all out.

Javier went on. "Another verse that destroys this confusing doctrine is Colossians 1:15, where the apostle Paul says that Christ is 'the firstborn of every creature.' How can you say that Jesus is God when the Bible clearly teaches that He was born before every creature? Right here it says that He was born. Was God ever born? No, He couldn't have been if He is ultimate." (He said this with a sidelong glance at Sean, who winced at the sound of

> *Who is the image of the invisible God, the first-born of every creature.*
> ~Colossians 1:15

104

the word *ultimate*.) "Another verse along these lines is Revelation 3:14. It basically teaches the same thing as Colossians 1:15. And the phrase 'only begotten,' used primarily by John, also communicates this. All this teaches that Jesus was begotten, that is, He was created.

"Then there are all the host of verses that teach that Jesus is inferior to the Father. He says it Himself in John 14:28. 'My Father is greater than I.' Doesn't sound like sovereignty, does it? In John 5:19 He says that He can't even do anything without the Father. Doesn't sound like omnipotence, does it? Then He says that He doesn't know when He is going to return again, but His Father does, according to Mark 13:32. Doesn't sound like omniscience, does it? I can't imagine more damaging testimony to the doctrine of the Trinity than such verses as these.

"Also, in the Garden of Gethsemane, Jesus prays to God. Was He praying to Himself? No, He was praying to God. See, if Jesus is God, then He was praying to Himself in the garden, but that interpretation makes no sense. Before He dies, Jesus cries out that God has forsaken Him. Does this mean that God forsook Himself? No, God forsook Jesus. So Jesus can't be God. How can a person forsake himself? It's totally ridiculous.

The faithful and true witness, the beginning of the creation of God.
~Revelation 3:14

For my father is greater than I.
~John 14:28

The Son can do nothing of himself, but what he seeth the Father do.
~John 5:19

But of that day and that hour knoweth no man . . . neither the Son, but the Father.
~Mark 13:32

"Think about Christ's temptation in Matthew 4." Javier stopped talking for a moment and glanced intently around the room. "Jenny," he said shortly, "was Jesus tempted in Matthew 4?"

Jenny looked suspicious. "Of course," she said simply.

"That's a deadly admission," Javier said with a note of triumph. "God can't be tempted. James 1:13 says He can't be. So if Jesus was tempted, He can't be God. This is yet another impossible hurdle for the Trinity doctrine to overcome."

Javier went on. "And look at what Jesus says in Matthew 19:17. He tells the ruler that he shouldn't have called Him 'good.' Could God have said this? Is God going to tell someone that He is not good? No, this was an instance of the inferior Jesus humbly accepting His position and making it known to others. You should follow Jesus' perfect example and humbly accept God's Word on the issue of the Trinity. This confusing doctrine is obviously false. Because it is not taught in the Scriptures, it must be considered to be a doctrine taught by demons. 'God is not the author of confusion,' the Scriptures teach in I Corinthians 14:33; and since the Trinity doctrine is so confusing and unreasonable, it must be a doctrine taught by demons."

Javier stopped for a moment and took a few deep breaths. I was looking at my toes, and every once in a while I'd glance up. Javier certainly knew the Bible enough to back up his side. Throughout his monologue I found myself swimming in all the Scripture passages he was throwing around. I felt more confused than ever. I knew the Bible was the truth, but I felt as though the Bible was challenging something that I'd always believed it taught. The only other option was that, somehow, Javier was misrepresenting the Scriptures. I wondered how that could be since they seemed to back up what he said. After all, how could Jesus be God and yet not know when He was going to return? How could He be God and yet be tempted? I felt sick, and I wanted to leave. I rejected that option but then found myself confronted with Javier's resistless logic. Was Javier teaching the truth, and was I rejecting it? After a moment of miserable indecision, I decided to withhold judgment until I got further light.

Javier wasn't finished pounding on the doctrine of the Trinity. "People in Christendom often say that the Bible actually does have verses that support the Trinity doctrine. However, they misinterpret all of their proof texts. For example, in the King James Version, John 1:1 says, 'In the beginning was the Word, and the Word was with God, and the Word was God.' Well, unfortunately, that is a mistranslation. The word *God* at the end of the verse doesn't have the article in the original language. It should read, 'and the Word was *a god.*' The word *God* in Greek and Hebrew often was used to denote false gods or even people and angels. (See Psalm 8:5; 82:6; and I Corinthians 8:5.) Just because the word for *God* is used of Jesus proves nothing. It just proves that Jesus is a 'mighty one,' which is what the word literally means. The Trinitarians need to find an instance in the Scriptures where Jesus is called Jehovah. This would clinch their case that Jesus is God. But this they do not have because it doesn't exist.

"Let me discuss more of their so-called proof texts. In John 20:28, when Thomas sees Jesus as a resurrected spirit being, he admits to the Resurrection and calls out, 'My Lord and my God!' The Trinitarians say that this is a clear instance of someone calling Jesus 'God.' But it doesn't say that Thomas called Jesus 'God.' It just says that Thomas said it. He probably was just exclaiming in amazement or spontaneously bursting out in worship to Jehovah.

"Also, in Matthew 28:19–20, Jesus gives the Great Commission. He says to His disciples that they should go and tell people in all the nations about Jehovah. Part of the command is to baptize those who follow God. Well, Trinitarians say that the Trinity is true because the statement is 'baptizing them in the name of the Father, and of the Son, and of the Holy Ghost.' But notice that the verse does not teach anything about one God in three persons. It only says to baptize people in the name of the Father, Son, and Holy Spirit. This passage says nothing about a Trinity. To say it does is a classic case of reading into the text what isn't there.

"Anyway, I think I've gone on enough about the Trinity. As I said before, it is a doctrine of demons. You shouldn't believe it. A Trinity is not the personal, loving Jehovah; a Trinity is a monstrosity. Who wants to believe in a three-headed God?"

I shivered as Javier made his final statements on the Trinity. I noticed that Donald had a look of extreme distaste on his face, and Jenny just looked sad. I still felt sick, and I was glad Javier was finished discussing the Trinity.

Jim, who looked totally unaffected by Javier's statements, looked happily around the room. "Anyone have any more leads for our Fachmann?"

"Yeah," I said. "Javier, if Jesus is just a man, then how come the Bible says He created everything?"

"Well, Jesus did create everything. God created Jesus first as Michael the Archangel. Michael created everything else as God's helper. This is what it says in Colossians 1:16: 'by means of him all [other] things were created in the heavens and upon the earth.' To provide the atonement, Michael became a man; he was born as the human child Jesus."

"OK, Javier," Jenny said, "what do you believe about the atonement of Christ? If Jesus isn't God, then how could He die for all men's sins?"

Javier nodded his head. "The atonement is a very misunderstood event. The problem is that people think that Jesus died for all men's sins. He didn't. He was a corresponding ransom for the sin of Adam, though Adam himself does not receive the benefits from it because Adam was a willful sinner, unlike most of the rest of mankind. The sinless Jesus died on the torture stake to remove the effects of Adam's sin and thus to free those who love God from the effects of Adam's sin."

"Hold on," I interrupted. "Did you say 'torture stake'? What about the cross?"

"Oh, the cross is an ancient pagan symbol. He didn't die on a cross. It was a straight pole Jesus was nailed to. The word translated *cross* in the Bible really just means a straight pole. Later, apostate

Christianity borrowed the symbol of the cross from paganism and added it to the true message."

"Oh," I said. *Weird,* I thought.

Javier went on. "The man Jesus died on the torture stake for the man Adam's sin. If Jesus had been anything other than a man, His payment would not have been in accordance with God's strict justice. If Jesus is God, then the payment would have far outweighed the cost. The cost was the death of a man. The death of God would have been a vast overpayment and would have failed to meet the strict demands of God's justice. Thus, this is another argument that Jesus could not be God. The atonement was the man Jesus paying for Adam's sin."

"OK, but what about all the rest of our sins? Did Jesus die for those too?" This was me.

"Well, Jesus died for Adam's sin that keeps you from eternal life. If you accept in faith Christ's atonement on your behalf, you will benefit from the atonement."

"I think we need to make it simple," Jenny said. "Just tell me if I'll be saved if I accept Jesus as my Savior."

"That depends on what you mean by that," Javier said. "If you believe in Christ, you will benefit from the atonement; that is correct. But only those who continue to believe and thus obey to the end will be able to enter the kingdom. As one of our books, *Let God Be True,* puts it, 'All who by reason of faith in Jehovah God and in Christ Jesus dedicate themselves to do God's will and then faithfully carry out their dedication will be rewarded with everlasting life.' Salvation is not something that a person experiences now. It is something the faithful will experience if they endure to the end."

"Really," Jenny said with a strange sound in her voice. "It sounds like enduring to the end is very important. How does one do it?"

"Well, after baptism you must set and achieve spiritual goals for yourself. You need to read your Bible every day. You need to attend congregation meetings and speak up for the encouragement of Jehovah's people. Learn to pray better. Let God's active force produce its fruitage in you: love, joy, peace, longsuffering, etc. Find joy in preaching the kingdom on doorsteps in your area. People who do these things are destined to survive the outpouring of God's wrath upon this system of things."

"Does a person have to be a member of the Jehovah's Witnesses to be saved?" Jenny asked.

"All adherents to other religious systems will be destroyed at the Battle of Armageddon, and no one can really understand the Scriptures without the help of the Watchtower literature; so, yes, you must bring yourself into the protective fold of the Jehovah's Witnesses. After all, they are members of the only true organization of God on earth."

"Javier, why don't you tell us what is going to happen when God judges this system of . . . whatever." Of course, me.

"That's *system of things.* It refers to the present age. What will happen at the end of it is very exciting. You see, when the Babylonian captivity began in 607 B.C., it was prophesied by Daniel that seven periods of time would elapse until the end. These seven periods of time were each 360 years. When you add up seven periods of 360 years, you get 2520 years. If you consider the year 607 B.C. as the starting point, the 2520 years end in A.D. 1914. It was in 1914—the year, by the way, when World War I began—that Christ came back invisibly. This indicates that Christ will soon destroy this system of things and set up a paradise on earth for the faithful. The beginning of the time of distress began in 1914, which explains why the time ever since then has been the bloodiest time in history.

"When Christ finally fights the Battle of Armageddon, He will destroy all the forces of evil. Then apostate Christendom will finally meet its just end! Christ will destroy everyone but God's faithful, who will populate a paradise on earth during the

Millennium. Jehovah's Witnesses from the past will be resurrected—men like Abraham, Moses, and Daniel. Also, multiplied billions of people will be resurrected to be given one last chance in the Millennium. If they learn God's ways and remain faithful, they will slowly be purified until the thousand years are over when Satan will be released for a short time. The resurrected host will be tempted at that time. Some will remain faithful to Jehovah. Others will reject the true God and follow Satan. These will be destroyed forever in the lake of fire. This is the second death, according to Revelation 20:14–15. The faithful will enjoy a paradise on earth forever.

"At that time Christ will deliver up the kingdom into Jehovah's hands. See I Corinthians 15:28. Every knee will bow and every tongue will confess that Jesus Christ is Lord, to the glory of God the Father, according to Philippians 2:10–11. And Jehovah's Witnesses will worship God for eternity."

"Hold it," Jenny said. "I've heard something about a remnant of 144,000, and they're the only ones who get to go to heaven. What you're saying now seems to contradict that."

"Well, no. I just haven't been as specific as maybe I should have been. The 144,000 of Revelation chapters 7 and 14 are Christ's body, what you would call 'the church.' They are the ones who have been born again. They're the remnant, the ones who will be joint-heirs with Christ. The quota for the 144,000 was filled in the early 1900s, and there were only a few thousand of them left alive by the year 2000. They will be resurrected in spirit bodies like Jesus was and will go to heaven. All the other Jehovah's Witnesses, sometimes known as *Jonadabs,* will enjoy everlasting peace and fulfillment in a paradise on earth."

"Well, that's a new one," I said. "What about those who don't follow Jehovah in the Millennium? You said they go to hell forever, but one of your Witnesses once told me that God doesn't send people to hell forever."

"True—they don't remain in hell forever. The doctrine of eternal punishment is another evidence of Christendom's apostasy and blasphemy. It impugns God's character to say that a God of love would send people to hell to burn forever. Who in their right mind would ever believe such a disgusting doctrine? No, when the fire of hell touches them they are annihilated, destroyed, as the Bible tells us. That is a just punishment for their sins. How can anyone say that burning people forever in hell is fair, no matter how many sins they have committed?"

"Well," Jim began, "we've covered God's purpose in history all the way through the fate of the individual. I think it's time to wrap it up."

"One more question," Jenny said. "You said that the 144,000 get resurrected 'spirit bodies like Jesus.' Could you explain that statement?"

"When Christ was raised from the dead, He was raised a life-giving spirit, according to I Corinthians 15:44–45. His body was not raised from the dead. He was resurrected spiritually. This is what all the remnant will experience."

"Nuff said," Jim pronounced, pushing his stool back from the counter. We all got up for a stretch. I grabbed my Bible and a soda and headed for the privacy of the classics section. I plopped into the saggy old couch in which I had spent so many evenings enjoying Dickens. I sat for what seemed like a long time, sipping my drink and mulling over what I'd heard. I was eager to hear everyone's evaluations.

Can We Comprehend God?

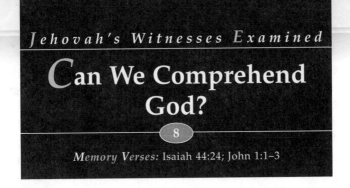

8

Memory Verses: Isaiah 44:24; John 1:1–3

I finished my soda just as Jim called us all back. I dragged myself out of the old couch in the classics section and went to the meeting area and was nearly swallowed up by one of Jim's orange chairs.

"You need some new furniture, Jim," I said. "It's all fun and games until someone gets hurt."

"Very funny," Jim said. "You're supposed to sit on the couch."

"Only slightly less dangerous," I said as I switched.

"Oh, just pick your next Fachmann, Steve," Jim said with a wry grin.

I asked Donald if he wanted to go first, but he was jotting some things down on paper and asked to go last. I looked at Hamid, remembering how good he had been on Mormonism. "Hamid, would you like to tell us your thoughts?"

Hamid nodded his head slowly and smiled. He looked at Javier. "You said that the doctrine of torment in hellfire is 'disgusting.' Yet I know from your own Bible that it is taught. And it most certainly is taught in the glorious Koran. On what basis do you assert that God will not allow men to burn?"

"On the basis that it is unthinkable. The God who would do such a thing is definitely not a God of love as Jehovah is. Besides, the Bible teaches that people are not conscious after death, so torment in a lake of fire is out of the question. Take a look at the clear statement of this in Ecclesiastes 9:5. It says, 'As for the dead, they are conscious of nothing at all.' This must mean that people don't have an immaterial side to their natures. They don't have a 'spirit,' as you would say."

"So how do you interpret the host of passages in your Scriptures that describe hellfire and torment?"

Jenny broke in at this point. "Yes, what about the passage in Luke 16, where the rich man and the beggar Lazarus die, and the rich man goes to a place where he is tormented in fire? It seems like that passage ought to make you rethink your position."

Luke 16:19–31

19 There was a certain rich man, which was clothed in purple and fine linen, and fared sumptuously every day: **20** And there was a certain beggar named Lazarus, which was laid at his gate, full of sores, **21** And desiring to be fed with the crumbs which fell from the rich man's table: moreover the dogs came and licked his sores. **22** And it came to pass, that the beggar died, and was carried by the angels into Abraham's bosom: the rich man also died, and was buried; **23** And in hell he lift up his eyes, being in torments, and seeth Abraham afar off, and Lazarus in his bosom. **24** And he cried and said, Father Abraham, have mercy on me, and send Lazarus, that he may dip the tip of his finger in water, and cool my tongue; for I am tormented in this flame. **25** But Abraham said, Son, remember that thou in thy lifetime receivedst thy good things, and likewise Lazarus evil things: but now he is comforted, and thou art tormented. **26** And beside all this, between us and you there is a great gulf fixed: so that they which would pass from hence to you cannot; neither can they pass to us, that would come from thence. **27** Then he said, I pray thee therefore, father, that thou wouldest send him to my father's house: **28** For I have five brethren; that he may testify unto them, lest they also come into this place of torment. **29** Abraham saith unto him, They have Moses and the prophets; let them hear them. **30** And he said, Nay, father Abraham: but if one went unto them from the dead, they will repent. **31** And he said unto him, If they hear not Moses and the prophets, neither will they be persuaded, though one rose from the dead.

Javier responded immediately. "It doesn't make me rethink my position at all. All Jesus' stories have metaphorical elements in them. It is not describing a literal place of torment but the torment that the Jews felt as they were confronted with Jesus' teaching. By rejecting the teaching, the Jews died spiritually, and the spiritual blessings of Jesus' teaching went to the poor, like the Lazarus character. The Jews were left to find torment in the very same teachings that were such a blessing to the poor."

Hamid spoke up again. "This is a very spiritualized interpretation of a well-known text from the Injil. I don't believe you are taking it at face value. But the Koran settles the issue. In Surah 25:11–14, the prophet says, 'For those who deny (the coming of) the Hour We have prepared a flame. When it seeth them from afar, they hear the crackling and the roar thereof. And when they are flung into a narrow place thereof, chained together, they pray for many destructions!' " Hamid closed his Koran and leaned back in his chair.

Jenny spoke up again. "I totally agree with Hamid's statement that you aren't taking Luke 16 at face value."

Javier smiled smugly. "Well, I haven't heard any of you deal with the passage from Ecclesiastes. You're ignoring a verse that would help you properly interpret those other passages."

There was a momentary pause as everyone took in the last exchange. Jenny was hunting for something in her Bible. Moments dragged by, so I looked around and saw Sean looking eager to ask a question. "Sean, would you like to go next?"

"Yes, thanks, Sucher," he replied. "Javier, how do you know that your organization is really God's? You said that it had to be God's true organization because you emphasize things like God's name. But don't other religious organizations emphasize things that are true about God? Of course they do."

Javier looked confident. "The apostate religions don't emphasize God's name like we do, but rather they obscure it."

Sean replied quickly. "But you assume that you are the ones who get to determine what the standard is for judging. Yes, God wants people to know that He is Jehovah, but is that fact really *the* standard by which to judge which organization is God's true one? No, I don't think so. I think it's an artificial standard by which to judge."

"So what *is* the standard, Sean?" Javier asked stiffly.

"Well, it's just like what I said when you were all grilling me. The Church of Jesus Christ of Latter-day Saints has a direct line to God through the office of prophet, seer, and revelator. And that office is active today. I'm sorry, but that beats your claims based on subjective analogies from the Old Testament."

Javier barely let Sean finish his statement. "You can say that after everything I said about your church's changing its mind? You may have what you call a prophet, seer, and revelator, but with a prophet like that, who needs false prophets?"

"OK, OK," Jim interjected loudly with warning glares at the two.

"All right, I'm done," Sean said a little sulkily.

"Sucher, let the next Fachmann speak," Jim said. I looked at Shlomo.

"Well," Shlomo began, "I actually would like to pick up where Sean left off. I don't agree with Sean's conclusion, but I wholeheartedly agree with his statement that the Witnesses are choosing a false standard to determine which is God's true organization. By the way, I'm beginning to hate that word *organization;* can we call it something else?"

"How about *church?*" Jenny suggested.

"Too Christian," Shlomo said, grimacing. "I'll just go with *group.* Anyway, I know what God's name is, and I don't go around profaning it by speaking it. And I especially wouldn't say it without considering its significance. A name in ancient times signified something. And when God communicated His name to Moses in the Torah, He wanted to communicate meaningful content, not just a label. You don't come to know a person by knowing the label that is his name. You come to know a person by learning all about him by observing him in different situations. Once you have experienced his reactions, his spontaneous expressions of emotion,

They play the same monotonous note. . . .

the way he relates to others, you can say you have begun to know him. You can begin to attach meaningful content to the label. But whenever I hear these Witnesses talk, they emphasize the label over meaningful content. They play the same monotonous note about God's name and how everyone is obscuring it. But *they* obscure the content by emphasizing the label. So, my question, Javier, is this: What to you is the significance of God's name?"

"Well, the name of Jehovah symbolizes who God is. He is not a Trinity. It does not matter how you pronounce the name; it is God's name, and it is by this name that we are to know this God. It is by this name that we are able to distinguish between the true God and false gods."

Shlomo smiled cynically. "You are supporting my observation, Javier. You obviously don't spend a lot of time meditating on the greatness of God. You're too busy trying to prove some inane point. You never sound like you enjoy God as the all-powerful Creator of the universe. You drone on and on about His name, but you don't seem to revere Him as the omnipotent and omniscient Ruler of the universe, who will reward those who obey Him and punish those who disobey. You don't glory in God as near, caring, and compassionate, careful to meet His creatures' needs, taking no delight in death and suffering—even when it is deserved. A group that is so sterile in its approach must be considered seriously deficient."

Shlomo noticed that Javier didn't respond, so he decided to plow ahead. "I also would like to question you concerning your belief that man has no immaterial side to his being. I noticed that you used Ecclesiastes 9:5 to support that. But Ecclesiastes 12:7 says, 'The spirit will return to God who gave it.' "

Javier smiled confidently. "I was hoping someone would bring that up. Can't the Hebrew word for *spirit* mean 'breath'?"

Shlomo looked a little taken off-guard. But he nodded.

Javier was quick to respond. "Then that verse doesn't change anything. It means that the breath or life that God breathed into man will return to God. It's a poetic way of saying 'he will die.' The word *spirit* in Scripture never refers to an immaterial man."

Shlomo looked momentarily surprised. "OK, you *may* be correct about that verse, but there are other passages that indicate that there is a material and an immaterial side to man. Isaiah 10:18 speaks of 'both soul and body.' This tells me that there is a difference between man's material and immaterial sides. I think that verse makes your position difficult."

Jenny jumped in at this point. She had her Bible open and had two or three fingers wedged in at various places to keep verses ready. "Here are just a couple verses that totally debunk your ideas, Javier. Matthew 10:28 speaks of God destroying 'both soul and body in hell.' And II Corinthians 5:6–8 says that 'to be absent from the body' is 'to be present with the Lord.' That sounds as though there's an immaterial side to human nature."

"Sucher, I guess we need to give the floor to Donald since the others seem to be done," offered Jim after a long silence.

"OK. Donald, I hope you say something about the Trinity," I suggested.

Donald nodded and answered. "Yes, Steve, I plan on focusing on the Trinity, including Christ's deity." Then he looked at Javier. "I've noticed before that Jehovah's Witnesses like to swamp their opponents with information. Your presentation sure confirmed that. I don't have time to deal with every can of worms you opened, but I will try to deal sufficiently with these issues for now. I plan on dealing with the atonement and salvation in my own presentation. I'll probably never even get to your problems with the end times." He stopped for a moment. "Javier, do you think you considered all the evidence in your discussion of the Trinity?"

"No, I didn't have time. But if I did, I'd be able to really show that doctrine for what it is."

Donald smiled. "Javier, your organization focuses only on part of the evidence. Let me support this by showing that your arguments don't necessarily prove your point and by showing you some biblical data that you didn't consider.

"Let's look at your arguments. They fall into some easily defined categories. First, you have statements that sound as though Jesus was created. I think you mentioned Colossians 1:15 and Revelation 3:14. Second, you have statements that seem to communicate that Jesus is limited in some way. You mentioned John 14:28, John 5:19, Mark 13:32, and Matthew 4. These texts, you said, indicate that Jesus is not as great as the Father, that Jesus is not sovereign, that He is not omniscient, and that He is not free from temptation. Third, you mentioned texts that seem logically contradictory. In these texts, if Jesus is God, you would have God praying to Himself, crying out to Himself, and forsaking Himself. Finally, you attacked some proof texts, such as John 1:1; 20:28; and Matthew 28:19–20. Is that it?"

"You forgot John 17:3. It decimates your position. Interesting that you left it out."

Donald's Rebuttal

GET THE BIG

PICTURE

I. Donald evaluates Javier's arguments
  A. Statements that sound as though Jesus was created
  B. Statements that communicate that Jesus is limited
  C. Texts that seem logically contradictory if Jesus is God

II. Donald offers support for the Trinity and Christ's deity
  A. Christ, the object of our worship
  B. Christ, identified as Jehovah

Donald's eyebrows raised a little. "Let's begin with your texts that seem to say that Jesus was created.

"You mentioned Colossians 1:15 and Revelation 3:14. Colossians 1:15 says Christ is 'the firstborn of every creature.' The word *firstborn* in modern English has only one meaning, and it implies that there was a time when the one described as 'born' did not exist. However, in the ancient world the word *firstborn* could also mean something else. This other meaning is seen in some Old Testament verses, especially Psalm 89:27. God says of King David, 'I will make him my firstborn, higher than the kings of the earth.' Here the word has the idea of preeminence. God planned to exalt David to preeminence, the status of a firstborn son over his brothers."

"But how do we know Colossians 1:15 means this?" I asked. I didn't see how all this about David could clinch the case.

"Good question, Sucher," Donald answered. "The way to find out is to look at the context and discern which meaning fits it better." Donald opened his Bible. "Notice that the verses immediately following verse 15 discuss Jesus' status as Creator of all things, as the preexistent One before all things, and the One who holds all things together. The end of verse 18 explicitly mentions Christ's preeminence. Now let's look at the general flow of the first two chapters. Paul argues that in Christ is all fulness (1:19), in Christ 'are hid all the treasures of wisdom and knowledge' (2:3), 'all the fulness of the Godhead' dwells in Christ (2:9), we need nothing else but Christ (2:10), and so on. As you can see, Paul is talking about the greatness and transcendence of Christ.

Colossians 1:15–18

15 Who is the image of the invisible God, the firstborn of every creature: **16** For by him were all things created, that are in heaven, and that are in earth, visible and invisible, whether they be thrones, or dominions, or principalities, or powers: all things were created by him, and for him: **17** And he is before all things, and by him all things consist. **18** And he is the head of the body, the church: who is the beginning, the firstborn from the dead; that in all things he might have the preeminence.

Therefore, the context indicates that the idea of preeminence is being communicated by the word *firstborn*."

"Wow," I said. "But what about the Revelation passage?"

Donald continued. "Revelation 3:14 is similar to Colossians 1:15. It uses a different Greek term that means 'beginning' or 'starting point.' But it also can mean 'source' or 'origin' or even 'ruler.' The verse could mean that Jesus is the source of Creation. This fits well with John 1:3: 'All things were made by him.' "

Donald went on. "OK, next let's discuss the verses that indicate Christ's limitations—John 14:28, John 5:19, Mark 13:32, and Matthew 4. These passages prove that Jesus is subordinate to the Father and that Jesus is fully human.

"John 5:19 and John 14:28 teach that Christ is subordinate to the Father. He doesn't do anything unless the Father tells Him, and He calls the Father 'greater.' And this subordination seems to continue beyond Christ's earthly life. Revelation 1:1 says that Jesus received the message of the Book of Revelation from the Father to give to John, and I Corinthians 11:3 says that God is Christ's authoritative head. Also, the title *Son* implies subordination to the Father. But it is a *functional* subordination, not one of essence. In other words, Jesus is not less than the Father in essence, only in function. I Corinthians 11:3 shows that the husband is the head over the wife, just as the Father is the head over Christ. But does the wife's subordination to her husband mean that she is less of a human being than he is? Of course not. And neither is Jesus less God than the Father."

"OK, but what about Mark 13:32 and Matthew 4? How can Jesus be God if He was ignorant and was tempted?" I asked. I wanted to make sure Donald answered the rest of Javier's points.

"Those passages emphasize Jesus' humanity."

"You admit that Jesus is human? How then can He be God?" Javier asked.

"Mark 13:32, in which Jesus admits ignorance of something, does seem to crush the doctrine of the deity of Christ—but only to those who don't understand that Jesus has the characteristics of both God and man. While He was on the earth, Jesus was simultaneously omniscient in His deity and ignorant in His humanity. This is admittedly difficult to grasp, but Jesus is fully God and fully man. He has two distinct natures in one person."

"How can you believe such an unreasonable idea?" Javier said, shaking his head.

"We believe it because the Scriptures teach it. The Bible asserts both Christ's ignorance and His omniscience. Look at John 21:17. Here the apostle Peter says to Christ, 'Thou knowest all things.' Also, Christ promises in John 14:12–14 that He will answer our prayers. It would take an omniscient being to hear and answer the prayers of all the Christians in the earth."

"But He admits elsewhere that He doesn't know everything!"

"Javier, you choose to ignore the clear meaning of such passages because you cannot see that the two ideas can be reconciled. You see, Jesus has two natures, His nature as God and His nature as man. As a man He had all the sinless limitations of a man. He grew tired and thirsty, according to John 4:6–7. He could bleed. He could die. Do these facts preclude Jesus' deity? No, because He is both God and man, two natures found inseparably in one person."

"It sounds as if Jesus were a schizophrenic! That's revolting."

"I'll admit your statement is revolting. But Jesus is not as you describe. Just read the Gospels, and you'll realize that Christ's two natures do not make Him mentally imbalanced."

I had followed most of this and said, "Donald, it really does seem like Jesus must have two souls or minds. It seems like He is two different people."

"It may seem that way. But there really is no logical necessity that two natures could not reside in one person; it's just that we've never experienced such a thing, and so we're skeptical. Scripture clearly says that Jesus was ignorant of some things. But it also says that He knows all things. How do you reconcile the two clear statements? You can't say one is clear and the other obscure. They both are clear. One says He did not know, and the other says He knows all. You can twist one side of it or you can accept both sides.

And I for one do not want to turn a deaf ear to what the Bible says, so I accept both. How can it be, you ask? The person, Jesus, has two natures, two sets of attributes: one human and one divine. You would expect this when you read passages such as Matthew 1:18, 20, and 23. The human child, Jesus, was also God with us."

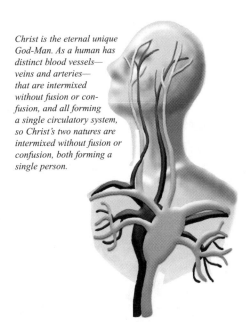

Christ is the eternal unique God-Man. As a human has distinct blood vessels—veins and arteries—that are intermixed without fusion or confusion, and all forming a single circulatory system, so Christ's two natures are intermixed without fusion or confusion, both forming a single person.

"So what about the issue of Jesus' temptation?" I asked. "Jesus' human nature was tempted, but not His divine nature?"

"No, I wouldn't put it that way. Jesus, the person, was tempted. The Bible never speaks of one of His natures doing things or experiencing things apart from the other nature. It just mentions the person of Christ doing or experiencing things. But if you want an explanation of how the divine Jesus could be tempted, then your answer most likely does lie in the fact that He was fully human. Jesus could be tempted because He was a human being, but Jesus never sinned."

"So, God was tempted," I said, trying to get used to the idea.

"I suppose that statement is permissible, as long as it is understood that the Son was temptable due only to His human nature. God, not bound to a human nature, is unable to be tempted, as James 1:13 says.

"Now let's deal with the texts that seem to charge Christians with logical contradiction. Javier claims that in these texts, if Jesus is God, you would have God praying to Himself, forsaking Himself, and so on. Well, these texts are difficult only if the Trinity is construed as modalism."

"What's that?" I asked.

"*Modalism* denies that there are three distinct persons in the Godhead. It says that there are three roles that one God plays like a single actor playing multiple roles in a play. How do we know that this view is wrong?"

Jenny spoke up. "We know it's the wrong view because of those verses Javier mentioned. How can we explain Jesus' being forsaken by God if He and God are the same person?"

"Exactly," Donald said with a look of satisfaction. "Javier, these verses you mentioned debunk modalism, not the Trinity, because the Trinity posits one God *in three truly distinct persons.* Christ could pray to God, be forsaken by God, and so on because He is God the Son—a distinct person from God the Father. These verses you mentioned are very important verses, but they do not contradict the Trinity in the slightest.

Views of God

Modalism
1 God
3 roles

Tritheism
3 Gods

Trinity
1 God
3 distinct persons

"Finally, you mentioned John 17:3, which says that the Father is 'the only true God.' On the surface this Scripture does seem to support your position. I mean, how can Jesus be the true God if the Father is the true God? Well, they couldn't both be the true God if Jesus and the Father were different in essence. In other words, they couldn't both be the true God if the Trinity were understood as tritheism. Tritheism certainly collapses under the weight of John 17:3. But the Trinity is not tritheism. All three are One. All three have the same essence and attributes; therefore, a statement about One's essence or attributes is necessarily a statement about the others' essence or attributes. So when the Father is called the only true God, the others are automatically called the only true God as well because the only true God is a Trinity."

"What?! It says that the *Father* is the only true God. Jesus can't be the true God." Javier's voice quivered with emotion.

"If the verse were to say, 'Only the Father is the true God,' you would be drawing the correct conclusion. Such a construction excludes the possibility of there being any other person but the Father who is the only true God. But the verse uses the word *only* to modify 'true God,' not 'Father.' It says that the Father is 'the only true God.'

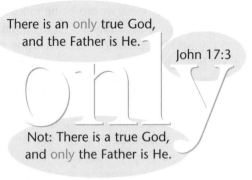

There is an only true God, and the Father is He.

John 17:3

Not: There is a true God, and only the Father is He.

In other words, 'There is an only true God, and the Father is He.' It doesn't say, 'There is a true God, and only the Father is He.' The construction does not deny the possibility of two other persons in the Godhead. And the rest of Scripture bears out that the Son and the Spirit are also God."

Javier looked confused and angry. "It still doesn't make sense! 'God is not the author of confusion,' according to I Corinthians 14:33. Therefore, this doctrine cannot be of God."

Donald wore a look of genuine compassion. "Javier, Jehovah's Witnesses use I Corinthians 14:33 to defend their rationalism. You think that it says that everything must make sense before you should believe it. But take a look at its context. Paul is correcting a church that held chaotic, disorganized meetings. God wants meetings to be orderly, not chaotic and confusing. This verse was never meant to guarantee that every doctrine will be fully understandable to men."

Donald went on. "Javier, you test everything by what makes sense to you. But that is rationalism, and it exalts the human mind over Scripture. Rationalism demands that the Scriptures conform to what the human mind thinks is reasonable. But when we consider the greatness of God, we are being more reasonable to doubt our own ability to understand everything about Him. For example, we can't grasp His eternality—that He never had a beginning and will never have an end. Our minds can't fathom it. But should we reject it because we cannot understand it? No. We should bow our finite human minds to His infinite mind."

Donald glanced at Jim, who was loudly tapping his watch, and quickly continued. "I wish I had time to discuss what you said about the Trinity proof texts. I will have to let them go and say only that you misrepresented the evidence. Now let me quickly present some biblical evidence that you overlooked in your presentation, Javier. One of the best arguments for Christ's deity is the fact that Christ is worshiped by men and—"

"I've heard this before, and I reject this argument," Javier interrupted, with disgust in his voice. "The Greek word translated *worship* can mean 'to honor.' It is used of men bowing down to other men and thus does not necessarily mean that expressions of honor to Jesus are equal to the depth of worship given to God."

Donald nodded. "Well, you are right about the Greek word, but your conclusion is wrong. Look at John 5:22–23. It says, 'the Father judgeth no man, but hath committed all judgment unto the Son: *That all men should honour the Son, even as they honour the Father.*' And look at Revelation 5:13." Donald quickly flipped over to that reference. "It says:

> And every creature which is in heaven, and on the earth . . . heard I saying, Blessing, and honour, and glory, and power, be unto him that sitteth upon the throne, *and unto the Lamb* for ever and ever.

"This passage shows every creature praising God and Christ with the same praise and at the same moment. I don't think anyone could ever convincingly say that the worship given to Christ here is less than that which is given to the

All creation is for Jesus Christ's pleasure, honor, and glory.

Father. Just look at Colossians 1:16, which says, 'All things were created . . . for him.' This means that all things were created to give Christ pleasure and honor and glory. It would be blasphemous to say this of anyone less than God. God alone deserves such an exalted position."

Donald took a breath and shifted gears. "Javier, consider John 12:37–41." We followed as Donald read aloud.

> "They believed not on him [Jesus]: That the saying of Esaias the prophet might be fulfilled, which he spake, *Lord, who hath believed our report? and to whom hath the arm of the Lord been revealed?* Therefore they could not believe, because that Esaias said again, *He hath blinded their eyes, and hardened their heart; that they should not see with their eyes, nor understand with their heart, and be converted, and I should heal them.* These things said Esaias, when he saw his glory, and spake of him."

"What's the point, Donald?" I asked, genuinely confused.

"It may be hard to see on the surface, but once you get it, it's as good as gold. John is explaining why many of the people couldn't believe in Jesus. He does this by quoting once from Isaiah 53:1 and once again from Isaiah 6:10. The incredible thing is that John the Apostle says that Isaiah said these two statements when he saw Jesus' glory. Now, Javier, whose glory did Isaiah see when he said Isaiah 6:10?"

"John says that it was Jesus' glory. Why are you asking me? "

Donald nimbly flipped some pages in his Bible. "Listen to Isaiah 6:1–5 and tell me whose glory it is that Isaiah saw.

> In the year that king Uzziah died I saw also the Lord sitting upon a throne, high and lifted up, and his train filled the temple. Above it stood the seraphims. . . . And one cried unto another, and said, Holy, holy, holy, is the Lord [the name Jehovah] of hosts: the whole earth is full of his glory. And the posts of the door moved at the voice of him that cried, and the house was filled with smoke. Then said I, Woe is me! for I am undone; because I am a man of unclean lips, and I dwell in the midst of a people of

unclean lips: for mine eyes have seen the King, the Lord [again, the name Jehovah] of hosts.

"These last two references to the word *Lord* are the Hebrew name *Jehovah*. So let me ask again—whose glory did Isaiah see in chapter 6 of his prophecy?"

Javier just sat staring at his Bible with a perplexed look. He began flipping pages back and forth.

"Woe is me! for I am undone. . . ."

Donald went on. "Look, Javier. Isaiah says that he saw Jehovah. John says concerning the same instance that Isaiah saw Jesus. I think the implications are clear: Jesus is Jehovah. Remember when you said that no verse in the Bible calls Jesus Jehovah? Well, this says it less directly than what you probably want, but it says it nonetheless."

Javier sat looking at his Bible, breathing heavy. "It still doesn't make sense," he said sullenly.

"Your opinion of what makes sense doesn't determine truth."

Javier's face hardened. He shut his Bible and looked away.

Donald leaned back in his chair and sighed. "The deity of Christ is taught in Scripture. It is the only explanation for the exalted position the New Testament gives Christ, who Himself asserted in John 14:9, 'He that hath seen me hath seen the Father.' "

"I think you've gone on long enough, Donald," Jim said with an edge in his voice. "I'm looking forward to seeing how you fare next time." With that, Jim dismissed us for the night.

Are All Men Depraved?

9

Memory Verses: Romans 5:12; Acts 3:14–15

It was hard to believe that the last night had come already. I felt like we had just agreed to do an Auseinandersetzung, and here we were, wrapping it up with Donald's presentation. But in another way, it seemed as though we'd been doing this thing forever. When I thought about what my life was like before these meetings (I had known very little about each religion, and the five Fachmänner—who by now seemed like old friends—had been complete strangers to me), I felt as though this was something that had been going on for years. Now that it was coming to an end, it made me a little sad.

Things started out in the usual way. We chatted with each other about insignificant things for a while. Then Jim spoke. "As you all know, we have been saving Donald's presentation for this evening. Normally, in our chronological arrangement, he would have gone after Shlomo and before Hamid. But our Sucher requested putting him at the end, no doubt because he wants to give his own ideas an unfair advantage." Jim looked at me with a smile, but somehow I could tell that his smile did not mean that he was kidding.

"Now," Jim continued, "I could dismiss this rearranging of the Fachmänner as inconsequential were it not for another very important fact: *Donald has dominated every night of our Auseinandersetzung.* Again, our Sucher has had no problem with this; indeed, he has encouraged it. Please understand, Sucher, I am not offended. But I do find the advantage that Donald has enjoyed to be a disadvantage for you, ultimately. You see, the purpose of all this interaction has been to get you to appreciate religions other than your own. I don't think you have come to that appreciation.

"So here's what we're going to do, Sucher. Tonight *I'll* be choosing who will cross-examine Donald and when."

"Wait a minute, Jim," Jenny said. "This whole thing is for Steve's benefit, not for you to make your case."

"I don't see how the two conflict," Jim said in return. "I want to help Steve *by making my case with him*. Now, of course, Steve may jump in and ask follow-up questions whenever he likes. But as I said, I will be calling on the Fachmänner."

Jenny looked dubious. "Jim, how is directing the cross-examination going to make your case?"

"Well, there is one other thing—we will not be giving Donald 'presentation time' this evening. It seems unnecessary to give him an hour to talk about Christianity's history and core beliefs since much of that has been covered during our discussions of the other religions. And, of course, much of that is already quite familiar to our Sucher. All it would do is shorten the time that should be devoted to grilling Donald."

"So," I said, "all we're doing tonight is having Donald defend his beliefs?"

"That's right," Jim answered.

"Wow. I thought you were Donald's friend."

" 'Faithful are the wounds of a friend'—as the old saying goes," Jim said, grinning at Donald.

"Yes, I've heard that 'saying' before," Donald said, answering Jim's smile with one of his own. "All I ask is that I have the liberty to answer fully every question that is posed to me."

"Of course," Jim said. "Now, let's begin with the rabbi. Shlomo, Donald is all yours."

"Thank you very much, Jim," Shlomo began. "Donald, let's get right to the point. In your attempts to refute those with whom you disagree, you have failed to respond to my rejection of the Christian concept of the human condition. I have asserted that since we are made in the image of God, we are essentially good ourselves. You, however, hold to a very pessimistic view of mankind. You claim, because you are a follower of the apostle Paul, that all mankind became evil because of Adam's sin. Therefore, everyone is basically evil. As I have said before, I find this teaching repugnant. It makes God an ogre because it states that God holds us accountable for the disobedience of another person. Also, I find this doctrine very dangerous. It teaches people that they are incapable of doing what God tells them to do. I say that God *commands* us to do good because we are like Him in His goodness, and we are therefore *able* to do good. You, however, think that God is remarkably cruel because He tells us to do what we *cannot* do. So my question to you, Donald, is twofold: Do you actually believe in original sin, and how do you defend this belief?"

"Yes, I believe in the doctrine of original sin," Donald began. He seemed relieved that his chance to defend himself had finally come. "As for my defense—well, that will take a few minutes. I trust none of you are opposed to my 'dominating' tonight's discussion?"

"You are certainly welcome to try," answered Jim (smiling again).

"First, Shlomo," Donald said, "I offer you the apostle Paul's statement in Romans 5:12: 'By one man sin entered into the world, and death by sin; and so death passed upon all men, for that all have sinned.' Now, in the context the 'one man' is Adam. So Paul is telling us that the entire human race became sinful when Adam—the father of us all—chose to disobey God."

"Well, obviously, I have several problems with what you've just said. First of all, I don't care what Paul says. Second, you have to—"

"Yes," Donald interrupted, "but you asked me to defend my belief, and as a Christian I must tell you that my first reason for believing in original sin is that the Christian Scriptures explicitly teach the doctrine."

"As I was saying, Donald," Shlomo continued, "before you can convince anyone here, you must demonstrate how God can hold all of us accountable for a sin we did not commit. Answer me that."

"I will answer your question with a question: Why do all humans die?"

Why do all men die?

Shlomo thought for a few seconds. "Because that is the way God has made the world."

"I disagree, and so does the Torah. The original creation was deathless. Death does not enter the world until Genesis 3, and it is presented there as *the penalty for sin.* If you claim that my position is untenable because it makes God unjust, then you have painted yourself into a corner, Shlomo. You then have to explain why it is that God punishes all of us with Adam's punishment even though He does not hold us accountable for Adam's sin. You see, this is one reason that Paul argues as he does in Romans 5. Paul is explaining why all people die—even little babies. All people die because all (even those too young to choose good deeds or evil deeds) are sinners.

"I should also give a brief explanation regarding the wording of Romans 5:12. Notice how Paul states the reason that all men die: 'For that *all have sinned.*' Paul does not say that all have received Adam's guilt. He states that all sinned. Somehow— don't ask me how—all of us were involved in Adam's sin. That day in the Garden of Eden *all of us sinned,* not just Adam."

> *Wherefore, as by one man sin entered into the world, and death by sin; and so death passed upon all men, for that all have sinned.*
>
> ~Romans 5:12

"That's crazy, Donald," Shlomo said. "Sucher, it's because of crazy explanations like this one that I'm not a Christian."

"Well, Shlomo," Donald jumped in on the end of his sentence, "at least I have an explanation as to why all humans die. And let me hasten to add that the problem of death is not the only problem you face when you deny the doctrine of original sin. Why does the Tanakh teach that all men are sinners if all did not become sinners in Adam's sin?"

"Because it is easier to sin than to do right. Another reason is that since Adam's sin, the human race has been covered by the cloud of a bad example. It was more likely that Cain would choose a sinful life because of his parents' bad example."

"I am afraid that your explanation will not do, Shlomo. If such were the case, then it would be possible for humans to live without sin. But no human ever has. Consider the lives of Abraham, Moses, and David. These are held up in your religion as three of the most righteous men who have ever lived. And yet David was an adulterer and a murderer. Moses was a murderer, and on more than one occasion he disobeyed God's direct commands. Judaism's great lawgiver broke one of the Law's most basic commands—he refused to circumcise his own son."

"Correction, Donald. He *delayed* circumcising him. Moses did it eventually."

"Not true. Moses' *wife* circumcised their son, and she did that only when God threatened to kill Moses for his disobedience. And then there is Abraham, 'the father of the faithful.' Several nights ago you presented Abraham as a man of remarkable character, someone who had the character to choose the one true God when nobody else would. I find this to be a terrible twisting of the Tanakh. Genesis does not present Abraham as a man of remarkable character. Abraham didn't reach out to God. God reached out to him."

"I would say that God reached out to Abraham because He could tell that Abraham was reaching out to Him."

"And I would say that you are wrong. Consider what Joshua said in his farewell address to Israel." Donald paused for a moment as he flipped through his Bible. "Joshua 24:2–3: 'Thus saith the Lord God of Israel, Your fathers dwelt on the other side of the flood in old time, even Terah, the father of Abraham, and the father of Nachor: and they served other gods. And I took your father Abraham from the other side of the flood, and led him throughout all the land of Canaan.' Abraham's continued propensity toward evil is seen in the fact that on several occasions he failed to trust God. As you know, Ishmael (and through him the Arab peoples) was born because Abraham sinned against God's promise."

There is not a just man upon earth, that doeth good, and sinneth not.
~Ecclesiastes 7:20

"And your point, Donald?" Jim threw in.

"My point is that if all men did not fall in Adam's fall, why is it that even the best men in the Tanakh were sinners?"

"I've already given my answer," Shlomo said, "but I'll say it again. They failed not because they were originally sinful but because they followed a bad example, and through following that bad example, they themselves became sinful."

"Well, that's not the explanation that David gives. In Psalm 51, the psalm recording his repentance for his adultery, he states that he sinned because he was a sinner. He did not say that he was a sinner because he sinned. And I quote: 'Behold, I was shapen in iniquity; and in sin did my mother conceive me.' If one of the Tanakh's best characters was himself conceived as a sinner, how can we claim that anyone is not originally sinful?

"And before you respond, Shlomo, consider these very important statements from the Tanakh.

"Genesis 8:21: 'The imagination of man's heart is evil from his youth.'

"I Kings 8:46: 'There is no man that sinneth not.'

"Ecclesiastes 7:20: 'There is not a just man upon earth, that doeth good, and sinneth not.'

"Isaiah 64:6: 'We are all as an unclean thing, and all our righteousnesses are as filthy rags.'

"Jeremiah 17:9: 'The heart is deceitful above all things, and desperately wicked: who can know it?'"

> The heart is deceitful above all things, and desperately wicked: who can know it?
> ~Jeremiah 17:9

"Donald," Shlomo said, shaking his head and shrugging his shoulders, "all you've done is demonstrate that the Tanakh teaches that all men sin. I have no qualms with that."

"But Shlomo, what I'm saying is that your explanation of why everyone sins is inadequate. If we all are born without sin, then surely someone—in all the history of the human race—would have resisted the temptation to sin and would therefore be perfect. But no one has. Doesn't that demonstrate mankind's problem is more fundamental than a bad environment and a bad example?

Doesn't this necessarily imply that all human beings are themselves sinful at the core? Indeed, doesn't the Tanakh explicitly say so—as I have demonstrated from Psalm 51:5 and Jeremiah 17:9?

"So, you see," Donald continued, "Paul's explanation in Romans 5 is not 'crazy,' as you have said. It is a confirmation of what we all sense throughout our reading of the Tanakh."

There was a momentary pause, and Jim looked at Sean. "Sean, Donald really let you have it before. Go ahead and make him squirm."

"Thanks, Jim. Donald, what you are saying is very dangerous. I know what Christians do with this original sin business. They use it to excuse their own inexcusable failure."

Donald responded without missing a beat. "And I will tell you, Sean, that if what I am saying is true, *your* position, like Shlomo's, is the one that is dangerous. I (by proclaiming the truth about man's sinfulness) am able to point people to their only hope—the mercy and grace of God. You, however, offer a damning hope built on lies. You tell men and women, who are by nature incapable of pleasing God, that they can please God. You convince them that they can be righteous in themselves, that they can work their way into God's favor.

> *The wicked are estranged from the womb: they go astray as soon as they be born, speaking lies.*
> ~Psalm 58:3

"And I ask you, Sean—and all of you, really—haven't you sensed in your own experience that mankind's sinfulness is innate? Sean, you have children, don't you?"

"Yes. Four."

"Have you ever had to teach your children to lie or to disobey? Of course not. It just comes naturally—even to those who are brought up in a loving, religious environment. And haven't we all learned from our own struggles that sin is woven into our beings? Why then would any of us try to deny that we are, in the words of David, 'shapen in iniquity'?"

During the moment's pause that followed, the answer to Donald's question suddenly hit me. Without thinking or hesitating, I blurted out, "Because we *are* 'shapen in iniquity.' "

"Exactly, Sucher! Perhaps the best proof of our own depravity is that we are so passionate about denying it. Because we are sinful, we are proud. And in our pride we detest the label 'sinner.' I am very glad that this line of questioning was chosen. You see, our disagreement over man's condition is perhaps our fundamental difference—indeed, I would say that it is the fundamental difference between my religion and all the others represented here.

"Each of you has a far more positive view of the nature of man than the Christian religion will allow. Now, Sucher, I want you to pay very close attention to what I'm saying here because I want to point out the basic differences between the false religions and the true religion. Shlomo says that men aren't born sinners: they rather become sinners through their wrong choices. Hamid denies that men are born wicked; he says they're just weak and limited. Sean speaks very highly of humanity: we're all literal children of God who can achieve godhood ourselves. And Javier, though he believes that Adam's sin is a problem, denies that men are inherently depraved and unable to please God.

"In so doing, Sucher, each of these religions reveals that it is *human* in its origin. These faiths are not concerned ultimately with proclaiming God's truth. They are concerned with defending the goodness of man. This is the fundamental difference between true religion and false religion. True religion seeks to justify God and God alone. False religion—human religion—seeks to justify *man*.

> *True religion seeks to justify God alone. False religion seeks to justify man.*
> ~Donald

This was one of the points that Paul was driving at in Romans 1, where the apostle explains (among other things) the origin of false religion. At this point, Sucher, I ask you to get a Bible and follow along with—"

"Hold on, Donald," Jim interrupted. "I am not going to let you turn this into one of your seminary lectures. I'm in charge, and I say that it's time to let Hamid—"

"It is true that you are in charge, Jim. But as the one in charge, you assured me that I would be able to answer each question fully. That is all I am trying to do."

"You've got five minutes, and then it's Hamid's turn."

"Fine. Now as I was saying, Romans 1 tells us about the origin of false religion. God reveals Himself to all of His creatures through nature and the human conscience. Verse 19 states that 'that which may be known of God' is displayed in the created order. Verse 20 explains what the content of this revelation is: 'Even his [that is, God's] eternal power and Godhead [or His divinity].' Verse 32 gives one more detail. It indicates that one of the things mankind learns about God's power, probably from listening to the voice of his own conscience, is 'the judgment of God.' So, what Paul is saying in this chapter is that through God's general revelation, all mankind perceives that God is great and powerful, and that He is justly angry with the human race.

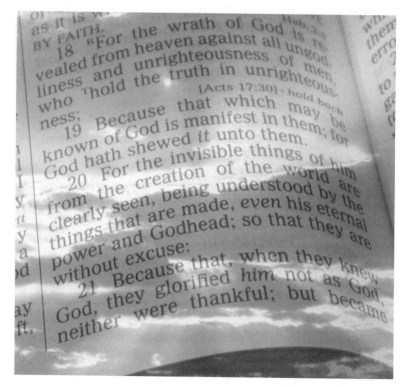

"What is man's natural reaction to this news? Consider verse 21: 'When they knew God, they glorified him not as God, neither were thankful; but became vain in their imaginations.' All men everywhere cannot bear the thought that they are as bad as God says they are. Rather than face the truth about themselves, they prefer not to glorify God as God. In so doing they become vainly infatuated with themselves. They would rather believe lies about God than believe the truth about themselves. And so Paul then says in verse 23 that human beings 'changed the glory of the uncorruptible God into an image made like to corruptible man.'

"And, Sucher, have you not seen this proved over and over again during these past several nights? Each of these religions has given some effort to making the leading human figures in their history look better than biblical teaching would allow. Shlomo described Abraham as a man of remarkable character. But the Tanakh speaks frankly of his sinfulness and failure. Hamid likewise puts much emphasis on Muhammad's honesty and goodness. Hamid dismisses the possibility of Muhammad's being deceived by his 'revelation' because Hamid considers Khadijah's advice to Muhammad—that Allah would not allow a man as good as he is to be deceived—as authoritative. This advice is ludicrous. Of course God would allow a man like Muhammad to be deceived—because, you see, Muhammad was not good. Like all men, he was fundamentally sinful—cursed with pride, selfishness, and hatred of God. Mormonism's founder, Joseph Smith, thought he was better than Jesus at keeping a church together. And the Watchtower organization assumes that no one can understand the Bible without its 'assistance.'

"Man—even religious man—is passionate about justifying himself and trying to defend his own goodness. This was the reason the Jews rejected their Messiah. Jesus told His disciples in John 15:22, 'If I had not come and spoken unto them, they had not had sin: but now they have no cloak for their sin.' If Jesus had come proclaiming the Jews' own goodness, they would have welcomed Him with open arms. But instead He proclaimed *God's* goodness, and like a bright light, Jesus' preaching, coupled with His sinless example, exposed them for what they were. Note also what Jesus said in John 3:19–20: 'This is the condemnation, that light is come into the world, and men loved darkness rather than light, because their deeds were evil. For every one that doeth evil hateth the light, neither cometh to the light, lest his deeds should be reproved.' And since they could not ignore Jesus' light, they had Him killed. Man would rather murder God's Son than face the truth about his own depravity."

"I'm not sure I can take much more of this," Shlomo said, looking at Jim.

"You won't have to," Jim said. "Enough, Donald!"

But Donald persisted. "False religion is not man's sincere attempt to please God. It is man's way of convincing himself that God is wrong and he is right."

With that, Jim came out of his seat. "Enough!"

The Christ of Derision, *Philippe de Champaigne*
From the Bob Jones University Collection

Things were tense—*really* tense. We all just looked at Jim for what seemed like a minute or two (even though it couldn't have been more than a few seconds). I definitely was not in the mood for a break. It was time for one, but I wanted to see where things were going to end up more than I wanted to stretch my legs.

Finally, Jim broke the awkward silence. "As I said a few minutes ago, it's time for Hamid to have a go at Donald."

"Donald," Hamid began, with a troubled look on his face, "I cannot tell you how offensive your little tirade against Islam and the great prophet was. You called Muhammad a hater of God. How can you ever hope to see peace and reconciliation in this world while you nurture such attitudes in others?"

"I do not hope to see the kind of peace you speak of, Hamid," Donald replied. "Peace at the price of truth is not real peace. It is my contention that our religions *cannot* be reconciled—not if we want them to remain true to their historical foundations. You cannot sincerely embrace Jesus as God's prophet and deny His deity at the same time. Jim brought all of us together for these several nights, wanting to prove to our Sucher that all religions are basically the same. Well, I think we've demonstrated they're not.

"Hamid, you have reproved me for being offensive, for calling Muhammad a God-hater. But not one of us can avoid offending the rest of the Fachmänner. You offended me and the Sucher when you told him that he was going to hell. We cannot be sincere followers of our own religions without being a serious offense to those who disagree with us. I think this demonstrates that Jim's thesis in all of this is untenable."

"Exactly, Donald," Jenny spoke up. "I've been trying to show this to Jim ever since I started working here. And I am—"

"I'd prefer you keep me out of this," Jim interrupted. "Hamid has the floor, Jenny. Let's keep it that way, at least for now."

"Jim," Hamid said, "my personal feeling is that Donald and I really have nothing more to say to each other. Several nights ago we learned that all of our differences come down to our disagreement on the issue of authority. I trust the Koran completely; Donald, however, trusts the Christian Scriptures completely. Whatever I bring up at this point will only carry us back to that fundamental difference.

"I will, however, conclude my part in this Auseinandersetzung with some words of advice for you, Donald. I fear that you so emphasize Jesus' role as the sufferer for the sins of the world that you end up perpetuating a misunderstanding of Jesus. Of course,

I do not believe that Jesus came to be a Savior at all. But I am not asking you to change your position in that regard— you would never listen to me if I tried. I will, however, urge you to give more emphasis to the fact that Jesus did serve Allah as a prophet.

"You see, your heavy emphasis on Jesus as the Savior of men leads you to undervalue the teachings of Jesus. I find this to be particularly tragic. Christianity's universal appeal is the moral teachings of Jesus. All men everywhere must admit that no one has ever taught as Jesus taught. His simple way of life, His self-sacrificing ways, His challenging exhortations to love God and man are remarkable beyond words. But, Donald, by emphasizing your Christian belief in Jesus' bloody death, you end up distancing people from those blessed teachings. People cannot get past your inordinate emphasis on *the cross* to what makes your religion truly uplifting and edifying. So my exhortation to you, Donald, is that you tone down your 'bloody Savior' rhetoric and reach out to other faiths by emphasizing Jesus' role as a great prophet of Allah—or *God,* as you would say."

"Hamid," Donald replied, "your advice grieves me. It shows the natural consequences of your commitment to defending your own goodness, which I talked about a few minutes ago. You cannot bring yourself to agree with God's assessment of your own depraved condition. What does your rejection of depravity lead to? *A rejection of the necessity of Jesus' atonement.* If a person doesn't think he is a sinner, he doesn't see the need of a Savior. Hence, you are happy to emphasize Jesus' prophetic role to the exclusion of His priestly role.

> *If a person doesn't think he is a sinner, he doesn't see the need of a Savior.*
> ~Donald

"But, as I have already demonstrated, the Bible teaches that we are all depraved and that we are therefore incapable of removing our own guilt or of pleasing God. This is why I cannot accept your advice to stop my 'bloody Savior' emphasis, as you called it. Jesus' moral teaching cannot be obeyed unless one has been saved from sin by His atoning work. When Christianity focuses on Jesus as teacher and not as Savior, it becomes a religion of the impossible. It ceases to proclaim the gospel—the good news that man can be pleasing in God's sight through faith in Christ's death on the cross. It instead preaches frustration and eternal misery. *Frustration* because it points people to a moral standard that cannot possibly be followed. *Eternal misery* because, as Jesus Himself said, 'Except your righteousness shall exceed the righteousness of the scribes and Pharisees, ye shall in no case enter into the kingdom of heaven.' "

"I take it, then, that you will not follow my advice?" Hamid said with a little bit of sarcasm.

"How can I, Hamid?" At this point Donald was definitely becoming emotional. He was not angry. He seemed sad somehow, as if he was about to cry. "I refuse to let my religion degenerate into a religion of works. Keeping laws cannot save any man because no man can keep God's laws. Let me remind you what Paul said in Galatians 2:21: 'If righteousness come by the law, then Christ is dead in vain.' If Jesus came only to teach us about God, why did He suffer that day at Calvary? God sent His Son to die for sinners—for sinners like me. By His grace, I will never preach His morals without preaching His suffering. I would be guilty of hideous ingratitude were I to do that. I would be failing to admit to the depth of my own wickedness, and I would end up saying that the most profound instance of self-sacrifice in human history *was not necessary!* It would amount to denying my Savior, Hamid. I—" Donald's voice cracked. He stopped, unable to continue.

Hamid looked uncomfortable at Donald's display of emotion, and he didn't pursue the questioning. He just sat staring with a perplexed look at Donald. After a few tense moments, Jim motioned to Javier.

Javier cleared his throat. "Donald, I, unlike Hamid here, do believe that Christ's sacrifice was necessary for our salvation. Christ replaced Adam's forfeited life and made it possible for men of good will to have eternal life. But your teaching about man's condition is irrelevant. You—"

Donald, who had regained his composure, interrupted. "Javier, I know you hold fiercely to what you believe, but your explanation of the atonement falls short of the biblical picture. You too see man as innately able to please God; thus, the idea that Jesus died for all men's sins is foreign to you. You don't see the need for Jesus to die for all men's sins because you don't see men as they really are—hell-deserving rebels who by nature despise and reject God."

Javier rolled his eyes. "People do good all the time, Donald. Don't paint the picture worse than it really is."

"Am I?" Donald asked sincerely. "Who cares if people are doing good all the time if they are constantly at their worst at the most important point, loyalty to God? Is the 'good' they do really good if they are rejecting God the whole time?"

"Are they rejecting God, Donald? Many are simply ignorant."

"Javier, every sin is a rejection of the God who wrote His law on human hearts. Every sin is an abuse of God's law, an attack on His character, a sneer at His goodness, and a raised fist of rebellion in His face. This sounds strange to people because God's perspective is so alien to us. But sin, even a 'little sin,' is blatant rejection of God's wisdom, way, and commands. It basically says to God, 'I think Your way is stupid. I'll do my own thing.' This is the biblical picture of man, Javier. This is why Job 15:16 says, 'How much more abominable and filthy is man, which drinketh iniquity like water?' And Romans 8:7 says that 'the carnal mind is enmity against God: for it is not subject to the law of God, neither indeed can be.' Since this is the condition of men, they needed a sacrifice 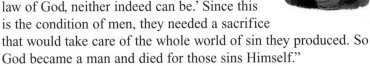 that would take care of the whole world of sin they produced. So God became a man and died for those sins Himself."

Javier spoke, shaking his head vigorously. "Jesus was not God. He was only a human being, taking Adam's place."

"Well, Javier, if you would admit the biblical view of man, then you would see that the payment wasn't only for one man's sin; it was for a world of sinners' sins. Peter says as much in I Peter 2:24 when he says that Jesus bore *our* sins in his body on the cross. And I John 2:2 says that Jesus' death was for the sins of *the whole world.* If Jesus were just a man, how could He pay for a multitude of other men's sins? And if all men have sinned as much as the Bible says, then there is a vast sin debt to pay. How can one mere man pay for all that sin? He couldn't. Jesus would have to be God to do it."

Javier looked at Donald blankly. "Jesus did not die for men's sins. He died to give a perfect human life to replace the life that Adam forfeited in the garden. That way, all the people who choose, love, and serve God can obtain eternal life."

"There you go again, Javier. You actually think that people naturally want to serve God, and Jesus' death provides them a way for their sincere love and devotion to count."

"Well, yes."

"That's my point. You reject the biblical view of man. Men are haters of God, Javier. They don't want to serve Him. They all willfully turn to their own way. It is because you reject this that you concoct theories of the atonement like the one you just explained. Yes, Jesus' death brings life, but it certainly does it differently from the way you think. Jesus didn't die for a world full of noble victims. He died for a world that hated Him. If you would accept this, you could see the true beauty of Jesus' sacrifice. Jesus actually paid the penalty for His enemies' sins, draws them to Himself, changes their heart so that they love Him, brings them into His family, and then eternally sticks to them closer than a brother. And this is even more profound when you consider that Jesus was the despised Lawmaker taking the punishment His own strict justice demanded. He was the One who had endured sin for millennia—men casting off His standards and chafing at His Word. And yet He, who by rights could have punished man, took man's punishment upon Himself. The wrath that would burn men's souls for eternity was snuffed out when the God-man died at Calvary."

> *All we like sheep have gone astray; we have turned every one to his own way; and the Lord hath laid on him the iniquity of us all.*
> ~Isaiah 53:6

"How can the infinite God be killed? It is foolishness!"

"It was the only way to pay for an incomprehensibly vast sin debt, Javier. How else would it all be paid for? Man couldn't pay it; he's helpless and condemned under the stringency of God's law. James 2:10 says if a man breaks one law, he is guilty of breaking the whole law. That is how exacting God is. He tolerates no sinfulness. And Jesus didn't stay dead; His body was resurrected, and now He ever lives to intercede for His people."

"Why do you have to muddy the waters and talk about all this sin? All that stood in the way of men's eternal life was Adam's sin. Jesus, the man, died to repay the life that Adam forfeited so that men who try to sincerely follow God could have life."

"I won't challenge your view of man again, Javier. That's becoming somewhat of a dead horse. Let me examine another aspect of your view. Your view implies that God manipulated one of His creatures to suffer and die for men while He Himself remained in His ivory tower. The Christian view is that God became a man, rent the eternal fellowship between the Father and the Son, and allowed Himself to be tortured for men. Your system presents an aloof God who is willing to help worthy men from afar. Christianity presents the living God who left the ivory tower, entered a world of woe, and became a man of sorrows—and that for His enemies! Javier, a person's love can be measured by the lengths he's willing to go for the benefit of another. Christ's death for sinners as explained in the Bible clearly displays a love that is more profound, more vast than we can ever hope to comprehend."

"I don't think so. Any God who would send people to hell forever is evil."

"Javier, you react so negatively to the thought of people being in hell forever because you don't see them as deserving it. People incurably hate the most valuable and glorious being in the universe. Their crime is infinite and deserves an infinite punishment. And God is not unloving for maintaining His moral laws. What do you want Him to do—alter the moral fabric of His very nature? To do so would be to forsake His own deity and to unmake the universe. Rather, God is relentlessly pursuing a spotless and sin-free universe. To set aside His views of sin and to fail to properly deal with it would be to invite sin to take its seat in His throne. You see, God must remain just so that He can guarantee that sin will finally be dealt with. It is His justice that allows us to say that there will be a resolution to the perplexing problem of evil and suffering."

I broke my long silence. "Why doesn't God just punish everyone then, Donald? Since man is as bad as you say, it makes sense that God would just wipe us all out."

"A logical question, Sucher. There is no doubt that God obligated Himself to condemn man to death. He promised Adam in the garden that the day he sinned he would die. But He didn't destroy men; He actually allowed men to perpetuate and proceed with history. So did He fail to administer justice? No, God passed over the sins of His people because He knew that He eventually would administer justice. He would punish those sins in Himself on the cross. The cross of Jesus Christ beautifully weds the justice and love of God. God loves men, and yet He will by no means clear the guilty. How can He reconcile these two aspects of His character? He became 'sin for us,' as II Corinthians 5:21 says. He made Himself the object of His strict justice. The cross forever communicates that God will never lay aside His justice. He actually suffered sin's penalty Himself rather than lay His justice aside. But the cross also communicates His love. He became the object of His own justice to save men from it. Those who realize their plight before the holy God and who place their trust in Christ's work on the cross for them will be delivered from their sins and from God's condemnation. In addition to that, God undertakes to transform the repentant sinner into His own image. Thus God's salvation is not only from condemnation, but it is also from the very practice of sin itself. Eventually, God will rule a perfect world of redeemed sinners, who will eternally worship Him."

> *The cross of Jesus Christ beautifully weds the justice and love of God.*
> ~Donald

Donald paused a moment, and things were deathly quiet in the room. "I think I have shown that the foundational difference between Christianity and these religions is their view of man, which has profound implications for their view of the person and work of Jesus Christ. And I think we all sense that the Bible's message as I've explained it is the way things really are. Christianity's distinct message lays bare the human soul like no other belief system. We all know that we are as the Bible describes us. This in itself is a powerful testimony that Christianity is God's truth. And Christianity is the only religion that offers a solution to the problem we all know we have." Donald looked around at everyone. "Many of you serve a God who claims to love. But how can you look into the face of Jesus Christ and say that you have ever known a love such as His? Hamid believes that the message of the cross is relatively unimportant and ought to be 'toned down.' But actually it's the only message of hope because it's the only message that deals with man's real problem."

Man's Problem—Christ's Solution

	Man's Depravity	Christ's Person	Christ's Work
Judaism	• Men are essentially good but weak and susceptible to bad examples.	• A man who taught valuable principles. • Some Jews: a heretic Jew.	• Christ was executed by the Roman government. • Some Jews: He got what he deserved.
Islam	• Men are limited and tend to be proud and self-sufficient.	• A man who was a prophet of Allah.	• Christ was crucified but did not die on the cross. God would not let his prophet be killed.
Mormonism	• Men are literal children of God who can achieve godhood themselves.	• Our brother, a fellow child of Heavenly Father. He achieved godhood in the pre-existence and provided the atonement.	• Jesus' death was to allow nearly everyone into one of the three kingdoms. It allows us to work for full salvation (godhood).
Jehovah's Witnesses	• Men want to serve God but can't due to a barrier from Adam's willful sin. • Christ's atonement restores Adam's free choice to all.	• An angel (Michael) who was born a man to provide the atonement for Adam's sin.	• Christ's atonement paid the penalty for Adam's sin so that faithful and obedient Jehovah's Witnesses can live in a paradise on earth.
Christianity	• Man's very nature is fallen and bent against God. Without divine assistance (grace), he cannot please God.	• God the Son incarnate as a man, whose two natures are united in one person: the God-man.	• Christ died to pay the penalty for His people's sins. Whoever trusts Him will be saved.

"OK, Donald," Jim said, "now it's time for me to ask a question."

"Certainly," Donald answered.

"Where will I go when I die?"

"Do you believe what Jesus said in John 14:6—that *He* is the way, the truth, and the life and that no one comes to God except through Him?"

"Donald, you amaze me. How can someone as intelligent and as well educated as you be such a prejudiced simpleton? I would be glad to call myself a Christian—as long as I can also be a Buddhist, a Jew, a Muslim, and all the rest. I am one with all of humanity, and I therefore have no interest in perpetuating the senseless divisions that people like you seem to be pressing on others. So what I'm saying is *NO!* I refuse to be put in a box. There are other ways to God. Christianity is not the only path."

"Then you will go to hell, Jim," Donald said calmly, looking Jim straight in the eye. "And let me add that it is not Christianity that you are rejecting. You are rejecting Jesus Christ."

"Oh really?" Jim said with a strange smile. "Then why do some of my Christian friends tell me I'll be fine in the next life?"

"All that proves is that people are fallible. It is possible for someone to claim to be a follower of Jesus and not represent His teaching accurately. Listen to Jesus Himself, Jim.

"John 3:18: 'He that believeth on him [that is, Jesus] is not condemned: but he that believeth not is condemned already, because he hath not believed in the name of the only begotten Son of God.'

"John 12:48: 'He that rejecteth me, and receiveth not my words, hath one that judgeth him: the word that I have spoken, the same shall judge him in the last day.' "

"Well, I guess that settles it. I'm going to hell. How about the other Fachmänner? Are you going to send them to hell too?"

"*God* judges the souls of men. Now concerning the others, the Bible teaches that as long as they continue to reject God's Christ, they are headed for hell."

"But how can you say that?" Jim's voice went up so high at the end that it cracked. "They love God too. They try to follow His teaching. They live good lives and—"

"Jim," Donald interrupted, "just consider what the apostle John said in I John 2:23: 'Whosoever denieth the Son, the same hath not the Father.' Those who reject God's own Son do not love God, do not follow His teaching, and do not live good lives. We have such a flaky idea of what it means to be good. We think that if someone appears kind and sincere, then he most certainly is essentially good. But, you see, that standard itself is another demonstration of our depravity. We judge the goodness of people by whether they are good to *us*. If they are friendly to *us* and kind to *us,* then they are good. But a far more important consideration is *God.* If the question is, How have these Fachmänner treated God? then we cannot describe them as good. They are unrepentant in their terrible sin of rejecting God's Son. They refuse to obey God's command given in John 5:23: 'All men should honour the Son, even as they honour the Father.' "

"And on that happy note, we end our Auseinandersetzung," Jim announced with a sarcastic grin. "Sucher, I hope you've learned a great deal, though I believe you would have learned much more if Donald had tried to be a bit more civil. Nevertheless, you have weathered the storm of our discussions, and you therefore deserve some recognition."

Jenny popped up and left the reading area for a second. When she came back, she had a framed certificate in her hand. Once she got back to the couch, she said, with a touch of formality, "We present you with this token for your good work these past several nights, and hereby we change your title from 'Sucher' to 'Fachmann.' We now welcome you to the honored ranks of the Fachmänner."

"Uh, this doesn't mean," I said, kind of stammering, "that I'm going to be called on to represent Christianity at future Auseinandersetzungs. I mean, I don't think I'm—"

"Life, Fachmann Steve, is an Auseinandersetzung."

I'm not exactly sure what happened next. I remember shaking hands and saying goodbye a bunch of times. But the next thing that I clearly remember is being outside. I was heading for my car, and I heard that slight Canadian accent saying something to me.

"What was that, Donald?" I asked.

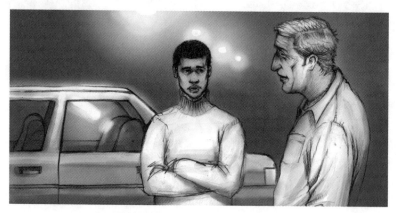

"I was just wondering how you feel about the Christian religion, now that you've heard a great deal about the others."

"I'd say that these meetings have really confirmed my faith."

"Oh Steve, I'm very glad to hear that."

"But I am still puzzled. If Jenny's right about *life* being an Auseinandersetzung, then how can I ever hope to talk with people from other religions in a way that will represent my own well? I mean, sure, you could do it. But that's because you're smart, you're fifty-something, and you've been teaching the Bible for a million years."

"It is true that there is no substitute for a life devoted to studying the Word of God. But, Steve, even now you can be very effective. Keep the main ideas in mind. What do you think the discussions' most important conflict was?"

"Well, there was more than one. Authority—you know, which holy book is right. Then man's condition. The atonement was pretty important. And then the Trinity, or Christ being God. It's hard to judge which was *most* important."

"OK, fine. What ties them together?"

My mind raced. "I don't think I can say."

"Well, man's depraved condition is presented in the Bible as the problem that the gospel exists to solve. The atonement is at the core of the gospel because it is God's way of solving man's problem. The Bible's authority is also important because it assures us that the gospel is true. And Christ's deity is vital to the gospel because it tells us that Christ's sacrifice was sufficient to rescue us from eternal doom."

"So it's the gospel that ties all these ideas together?" I asked.

"Right. And what is the gospel but the facts about the person and work of Jesus Christ?"

"But everyone in that room showed a lot of respect for Jesus."

"Everyone has great respect for aspects of Jesus. But no one in that room—except for Jenny, you, and me—believes all that the Bible reveals about Jesus. And, you see, this is the key to dealing with other religions in the world. They sound good and sincere initially because they talk about God. They talk about how great He is, how He made us, and how we are obligated to love Him and serve Him. But you begin to unmask these religions when you start asking them questions about Jesus. It is at that point that false religions expose themselves as false. Throughout the discussions, I had one question on my mind: What do they think of Jesus?"

"Boy, I sure wish Jim could understand this stuff. He seems so smart, but sometimes he just won't listen to reason."

"He can't, Steve. To 'understand this stuff' takes a miracle."

"That's the truth. He's about as hard as a person can get."

"That's not what I mean, Steve. Anyone who comes to Christ for salvation does so because of a miracle. Consider that famous passage in Matthew 16. Jesus asked His disciples what the people of that day were saying about Him. After the disciples stated that some thought He was Elijah and that others thought He was Jeremiah, Jesus put them on the spot and asked them who *they* thought He was. And, of course, Peter gave that memorable answer: 'Thou art the Christ, the Son of the living God.' That much most Christians remember. But many forget what comes next: 'And Jesus answered and said unto him, Blessed art thou, Simon Bar-jona: for flesh and blood hath not revealed it unto thee, but my Father which is in heaven.' People who answer correctly the question, Who is this Jesus? are able to do so because God has done a special work in their heart through the working of the Holy Spirit."

"So Jim needs prayer," I said thoughtfully.

"Lots." Donald had a wistful look and a smile on his face.

I got into my car and headed for home. *It takes a miracle,* I thought over and over again as I drove through town. And then it hit me: anyone who has experienced this miracle is *blessed* because Jesus said, "Blessed art thou, Simon Bar-jona." *Blessed are you, Steve, for it wasn't any human being that made you a Christian. The Father has made you born again.* By that time I was pulling into my driveway. "Life is an Auseinandersetzung," I remembered Jenny saying. "Don't worry," I said out loud as I shut the car door. "I'm ready for it. I've been blessed by God with the greatest miracle of all."

Photograph Credits

The following agencies and individuals have furnished materials to meet the photographic needs of this textbook. We wish to express our gratitude to them for their important contribution.

Bob Jones University Collection
Cartesia Software
Corbis
Library of Congress
PhotoDisc, Inc.
Saudi Aramco World
Bryan Smith
Carla Thomas
Utah State Historical Society
www.arttoday.com

Chapter 1
Bryan Smith 18

Chapter 2
Corbis 36

Chapter 3
Katrina Thomas/*Saudi Aramco World*/PADIA 41; Dick Doughty/*Saudi Aramco World*/PADIA 42; Photo Disc/Getty Images 44, 52; Cartesia Software (maps) 46 (both); Corbis 48; S. M. Amin/*Saudi Aramco World*/PADIA 53

Chapter 4
John Champney/*Saudi Aramco World*/PADIA 58; Cartesia Software (maps) 60; Photo Disc/Getty Images 64

Chapter 5
©2003-www.arttoday.com 75; Library of Congress 76, 77

Chapter 6
Torah Scroll from the Bob Jones University Museum & Gallery Bowen Collection of Antiquities 88; used by permission, Utah State Historical Society, all rights reserved 91; Corbis 97

Chapter 8
Photo Disc/Getty Images 126

Chapter 9
Corbis 132; Carla Thomas 138 (Bible); Photo Disc/Getty Images 138 (clouds); *The Christ of Derision,* Philippe de Champaigne, from the Bob Jones University Collection 140